ALSO BY TSOKNYI RINPOCHE

Carefree Simplicity

Fearless Simplicity

ALSO BY ERIC SWANSON

The Joy of Living (with Yongey Mingyur Rinpoche)

Joyful Wisdom (with Yongey Mingyur Rinpoche)

What the Lotus Said

The Boy in the Lake

OPEN
OPEN

OPEN HEART,
OPEN MIND

Awakening the Power of Essence Love

TSOKNYI RINPOCHE

WITH ERIC SWANSON

Harmony Books
New York

Published in the United States by Harmony Books,
an imprint of the Crown Publishing Group,
a division of Random House, Inc., New York.
www.crownpublishing.com

Harmony Books is a registered trademark and the Harmony Books colophon is a
trademark of Random House, Inc.

Library of Congress Cataloging-in-Publication Data

Tsoknyi Rinpoche.
Open heart, open mind / by Tsoknyi Rinpoche with Eric Swanson. — 1st ed.
p. cm.
Includes bibliographical references (p.   ) and index.
1. Religious life—Buddhism.   I. Swanson, Eric.   II. Title.
BQ5410.T79 2012
294.3'444—dc23   2011051557

ISBN: 978-0-307-88820-4
eISBN: 978-0-307-88822-8

Printed in the United States of America

Book design by Jo Anne Metsch
Jacket design by Jen O'Conner
Jacket photography by Chimey Yangzom

10   9   8   7   6   5   4   3   2   1

First Edition

For Chimey Yangzom, my wife

Contents

Contents

Foreword

If you want to find a fish, look in the ocean.
If you want to find yourself, look in your mind.

I first met Tsoknyi Rinpoche in 1997 in Litchfield, Connecticut. It was my first *dzogchen* retreat and I was quite excited and more than a little nervous. But there was nothing really to worry about. Rinpoche was such a fine and true teacher that he quickly put us all at ease with his wit, humor, and utter naturalness; at the same time challenging us over and over again to discover, and then rest in, the open truth of our natural essence, our original beingness. I've considered him a trusted teacher and cherished friend ever since. He's just one of those people you look forward to seeing and being with, whom one remembers with a smile and a laugh. It's always meaningful. Having studied under some of the giants of the Tibetan Buddhist tradition, most of whom sadly are now gone, Rinpoche is a powerful and eloquent link between the great yogi practitioners of old Tibet and our bewildering twenty-first century. He's completely comfortable in both. And he makes us comfortable, too.

Rinpoche has worked very hard to understand the peculiarities of the human mind so that he might more effectively help us break through our self-imposed limitations and seriousness. Lasting love, wisdom, and bliss are possible. But we can get pretty stuck in ourselves and our ideas.

Essence love is wide open and without bias. It's the freedom in a child's wild laughter, the soft warmth of well-being when we are happy for no particular reason. It is defined by Rinpoche as "unconditional kindness, gentleness, and affection born of openness and intelligence that can be nurtured into a bright, burning flame that warms the whole world." It's the joyous loving embrace of life itself—with all its craziness.

We can find it in ourselves because that's who we are. It is our birthright as human beings. Just as we have two eyes and two arms, we are this basic love. It can be covered over and confused such that we cannot recognize it or feel it. So we spend our lives chasing after it in relationships, money, power, things, and ideas—as if our inner loss can be found outside of ourselves. And maybe it can be momentarily. But eventually it just makes us feel hollow, exhausted, afraid, and angry. Somewhere in our hearts we recognize this, and in our most naked moments, we sense the emptiness and sadness that lies under the surface of our busy lives. Yet we yearn for so much more and sense deep down that true happiness is attainable.

This book dares us to find what we have temporarily lost and to begin a path of reconnection to our deepest nature, which is joyous, open, and free of all conditions and conditioning, like a cloudless and radiant sky. Recognizing our nature allows the warmth of compassion and love to naturally express themselves in everything we do. This path is not esoteric nor does it require some special ability. It is practical, logical, and clear. It is simply who we are. At root we all vibrate with love. We are love that has no limit and that can shine through every moment, whether we are happy or sad.

We may have met someone like this—some see this in the Dalai

Lama or Mother Teresa, or maybe in our own mother or father. They make us instinctively smile and feel a warmth that is uncontrived, natural. Why? Because they shine with a kind of selfless love and compassion that we recognize as our own true identity. This book can help us find that initial spark that will grow into a roaring fire. It's up to us.

—RICHARD GERE

A Note About Tibetan Words

Sprinkled throughout this book are some Tibetan terms that I've taken the liberty to transliterate in ways that don't necessarily conform to conventional, scholarly methods; a choice that will probably horrify many people who have devoted a great deal of time and effort into translating a language that is ripe with symbolic meanings. Many of the words used in classical and common Tibetan are loaded with silent consonants at the beginning and end of words, which sometimes affect pronunciation and sometimes do not.

Like many Asian languages, Tibetan has a tonal component. There are slight variations between many consonants and consonant combinations that strike fear into the hearts of many of the extraordinary people who serve as translators for Tibetan teachers. I've heard of a couple of instances in which a translator was asked to translate the Tibetan word for "ice," which, with one slight misstep in intonation, is the Tibetan word for "shit."

The teachers laugh their robes off at such uncomfortable challenges. Their laughter is not a form of cruelty but rather a gift, an opportunity to recognize and reconcile ourselves with the possibility that, however learned or successful we may be, we all make mistakes. Once we recognize them, we can learn from them and grow from them.

A Note About Tibetan Words

Many people have asked, after the publication of two books on which I had the honor of working with Yongey Mingyur Rinpoche, if I was the translator. Sadly, I had to disabuse them of that notion. My knowledge of the Tibetan language is limited to some ritual prayers and a few useful phrases, such as "I don't eat meat," "Is so-and-so here?," and "Where is the bathroom?" (or sometimes "Is there a bathroom?"). Buddha help me if I messed up the syntax or mispronounced, ever so slightly, a single word. It can be rather embarrassing to say "I don't eat a bathroom."

But Tsoknyi Rinpoche and the people who assist him in carrying out the tremendous responsibilities thrust upon him, at an age when many of us were concerned with sneaking cigarettes or alcohol off school grounds, have been very kind. They've taken great pains to assist me in understanding the subtleties of the Tibetan language and the wisdom expressed therein, which, in turn, expresses an understanding of the human condition and the possibilities of emotional evolution that is extremely precise and refined.

Of course, Buddhists have a bit of an advantage over some other people, inasmuch as they've been studying the actions of human beings and the impact of their decisions for more than two thousand years.

It has been an incredible honor to work with Tsoknyi Rinpoche, one of the kindest, most compassionate human beings I have ever had the privilege to meet. He's been straightforward in admitting his own mistakes, and has literally guided me with a hand on my arm through some of the understandings and processes described in the following pages. I hope that at least some of his extraordinary candor, warmth, humor, and humanity shine through in the following pages.

—ERIC SWANSON

ONE

The Bridge

A few years ago, I visited a pair of giant skyscrapers connected by a bridge made of thick, transparent glass. I could see right through the floor to the city streets hundreds of feet below. As I took a first step onto the bridge, my muscles froze. My heart started racing and I began to sweat. I was gripped by overwhelming terror.

"This bridge can't hold me up," I thought. "If I try to walk across it, I'll fall right through and die."

Paralyzing fear is not, perhaps, the response one might expect from a guy who was raised and trained in the tradition of Tibetan Buddhism and teaches and counsels people around the world.

I can't say much about other teachers' experiences. I can only say that I'm just as likely as anyone else to stumble upon conditions that frighten, confuse, sadden, or otherwise trouble me. I'm exposed to just about any situation that any other person might experience. Yet among the many lessons I've learned from my own teachers, my students, my family, and my friends, I've come to welcome such conditions as a means of understanding that simply being alive is a marvel. People around the globe have experienced severe hardships due to war, natural disasters, financial catastrophes, and political disputes, among other things.

Such trials aren't new or specific to the era in which we live. Throughout recorded history, people have faced many of the same sorts of challenges.

Yet the courage people have shown in the face of pain is a moving example of the complex wonder of being alive. So many people have lost their homes, their children, other family members, and friends. But even in their grief and pain, they express a willingness to go on, to recover or rebuild what they can—to *live*, not just despairingly, day to day, but with a sense that whatever effort they expend will benefit future generations.

WAKING UP

Learning to live with such courage presents us with the opportunity to see the nature of the challenges we face, the nature of ourselves, and the nature of reality in a radically different light—a process that the Buddha and the masters who followed in his footsteps likened to awakening from a dream, in which we experience things that are not quite true but that *appear* and *feel* true.

I'm sure you've had such experiences in your own life. Many people have told me of dreams in which they are chased by monsters, returned to homes that have many hidden rooms, or have engaged in odd situations with people familiar to them. When the alarm clock goes off, when children awaken from their own dreams and look to their parents for comfort and reassurance, when household animals bark, meow, or nuzzle to be fed, the dreamers are snapped awake to a somewhat different reality.

This sort of awakening may be abrupt and perhaps a bit disturbing. Thoughts, images, and feelings may linger for a while, like cobwebs waving in a breeze. If the dream was particularly intense, the cobwebs may linger longer, maybe haunting us throughout the day. We try to shake them off, and may eventually succeed in doing so.

SPINNING WHEELS

But even if we manage to do that, we end up trapped in another dream: the dream of conventional or everyday reality, in which we experience any number of fears and vulnerabilities that appear and feel quite solid and true, but which, upon closer examination, are neither as solid nor as true as we assume. This "waking dream" (of which ordinary dreams are also a part) is known in Sanskrit as *samsara* and in Tibetan as *khorlo*. Both terms may be understood as spinning around on a wheel that keeps turning and turning in the same direction.

Samsara is often compared to a potter's wheel. A potter throws clay on a wheel and shapes it using his or her hands and a great deal of talent while typically continuing to spin the wheel in the same direction.

Likewise, during the course of our own lives, many of us experience a sense of motion, a sense of making something or of making something happen. Unfortunately, as it turns out, what we end up doing is recycling the same old mental and emotional habits in different forms, using the same old technique of using whatever means are available to us to continue turning our mental and emotional potter's wheel. We keep thinking or feeling that "This time, the result is going to be different."

However quickly we spin, however skillfully we use our resources to create something beautiful or lasting, we're bound to experience a bit of disappointment. Our creations chip or break. Relationships fall apart. Jobs and homes are lost.

Recently I heard a quote by the great psychologist Carl Jung: "The whole world wants peace and the whole world prepares for war." In other words, what we wish for differs from what we're actually thinking, feeling, and doing. From the moment we wake up to the moment we fall into exhausted sleep, most of us are confronted with so many challenges: social, psychological, ecological, and economic. Given the current troubles of the world economy, the harmful effects of global climate change, the occurrence of natural disasters and epidemic illnesses, and the persistence of acts of violence by individuals and groups, the world in which we find ourselves can seem like a ticking time bomb, moments away from exploding.

Our interior lives, meanwhile, mirror the various dysfunctions of the external world. We've become experts at multitasking the possibilities of disaster. Our minds work like perpetual news channels, complete with big windows showing the main story of the moment, side windows showing stock and weather reports, and "crawlers" providing the latest, often sensational updates.

Or is it the other way around? Could the trauma evident on the world stage reflect a fractured internal image? A conflict between our longing for well-being, the urge to fight anyone or anything that threatens us, and the inhibitions of fear, loneliness, and despair we acquire when someone or some situation inflicts a wound upon our hearts that seems impossible to heal?

As human beings, we find ourselves in an uncomfortable position of balancing thoughts, feelings, and actions over which we can acknowledge some conscious control, and mental, emotional, and behavioral habits formed by factors beyond conscious awareness. For many of us this discomfort feels as though we're living a double life. A shadow seems to stalk us, a self behind the personality we consciously acknowledge and present to the world. Identifying and coming to terms with this shadow, for most of us, can be an unsettling experience. But the process does have its upside. A shadow is projected by some source of light, and by recognizing and acknowledging our shadow selves we can begin to trace a path toward the light.

SLOW AND STEADY

Discovering this light is a gradual and deeply personal process through which we begin to *see* the causes and consequences of our thoughts, feelings, and behaviors more brightly and vividly than we might previously have done.

As we engage in this process, a similar brightness begins to emerge in terms of our understanding of the causes and conditions through which the thoughts, feelings, and actions of others evolve. We deal directly with some of these people—our family members, our friends, our coworkers—every day. Others—business executives or politicians, for example—may not interact with us quite so closely, but their choices nevertheless affect our lives. Across the globe, for instance, people in boardrooms make decisions that have significant consequences on our ability to find or keep a job, pay our bills, or, in some cases, go to war. We don't know them personally and they don't know us, but their decisions have an impact on our lives.

Through some amazing breakthroughs in technology over the past few years, others produce videos, blogs, websites, and other forums of social commentary and interconnectedness that affect us in many ways—sometimes subtle and sometimes less so—inspiring awe, disgust, disenchantment, or emotional release.

Many people complain that in this era we suffer from "information overload." There are so many ideas, so many arguments, so many details flooding the world today, they say. I don't see this expansion in negative terms, however. Rather, I see it as an opportunity to learn and grow from this wealth of expressions and interactions.

Everything I've been taught, everything I've learned through my own life and through the experiences of teachers, students, and friends, points toward an innate capacity to learn and grow, to extend our ability to dive more deeply than we ever imagined possible into our own thoughts and feelings, and to treat the choices we and those we tend to see as "others" make with respect, courtesy, and compassionate understanding. I see it as a chance to become somewhat less judgmental, a possibility to open ourselves to perspectives with which we may not agree and toward which we may even feel some hostility.

However, if we engage in the process of opening to the possibility of understanding the role of the causes and conditions involved in our development as beings, if we engage in the process of understanding the thoughts and feelings that motivate us and those with whom we share our lives, we can begin to open our hearts. We can begin to love not only ourselves—which we think of as flawed or wounded—but also the beings with whom we share this planet full of wonders. We can begin to experience a warmth and a kindness we never thought possible.

LOOKING

Life is a challenge.

It's also an opportunity.

Moment by moment, day by day, week by week, year by year, we face a variety of obstacles that test our strength, our faith, and our patience. Often, we watch, helplessly and hopelessly, as we become slaves to international corporations, slaves to our bosses, to our friends and families, and to time. But we don't have to endure this bondage. We can set out on a path that allows us to reconnect with a tremendous inner potential for openness, warmth, and wisdom. Doing so, however, involves taking a fresh view of whatever circumstances we face, whether that involves chronic illness, childhood pain, relation-ship difficulties, or the loss of a job or a home. Although the message I was taught was inspired by a man who lived twenty-five hundred years ago, it remains as fresh today as it was back then.

What is that message?

Look at your life. Look at the ways in which you define who you are and what you're capable of achieving. Look at your goals. Look at the pressures applied by the people around you and the culture in which you were raised. Look again. And again. Keep looking until you realize, within your own experience, that you're so much more than who you believe you are. Keep looking until you discover the wondrous heart, the marvelous mind, that is the very basis of your being.

In the particular situation of crossing the glass bridge, described earlier, I took what I'd learned about *looking* quite seriously. Instead of taking some other route, I stepped back to look across the bridge and saw many people walking back and forth across it. Some were even hauling hand trucks loaded with heavy boxes. They appeared cheerful and unworried, just going about their business.

"Why then," I wondered, "am I so scared?"

After a few moments, the "why" hit me.

As a child, I'd taken a lot of risks, climbing to the tallest tree branches and scrambling onto mountain overhangs that even goats feared to climb. In the course of my adventures I'd taken my share of spills and the pain I'd felt had imprinted itself on my physical body. The physical pain generated a fearful emotional response to the possibility of falling. Taken together, these physical and emotional responses then crystallized into an idea that heights are dangerous.

In simple terms, a pattern had evolved: a tightly woven knot of phys-ical, emotional, and conceptual reactions which, taken together, I'd accepted as fact, a bit of truth about who I was and the circumstances in which I found myself. The first time I'd tried to step onto the bridge, my pattern had taken over completely. I had become my fear. My fear had become me.

"Okay," I told myself, "I can see a pattern here, but does this pattern apply right here and now?"

Of course not. The glass was solid. Other people were walking across the bridge. The pattern made no intellectual sense. I tried a second time to step onto the bridge—and failed again. Even though I knew intellectually that I wouldn't fall, I still froze.

So I stepped back once more and began to look again at what was holding me back. After a few minutes' consideration, I realized that the pattern of fear had become so deeply embedded in my thoughts, feelings, and physical sensations that I'd come to accept it as part of me, of who I believed I was and how I defined the world around me. This sort of identification is the "glue" that holds patterns together.

KINDNESS

But after this first recognition, I realized something even more important. I was being unkind to my pattern. I wanted to get rid of it, to just break through it right away without taking any time to listen to it or learn from it.

Patterns, you see, often take awhile to build up, and it can take a while to see them, understand them, and loosen the knots that form them. Working with our patterns requires great kindness and gentleness: the same qualities parents apply when they comfort children crying in the dark. As a parent myself, I've learned that dealing with children in distress often involves diving deeply into one's own heart and finding a way to communicate to them that their fears and discomfort are okay—while at the same time letting them know that fear, cold, dampness, or hunger are temporary conditions that don't define who they are.

Applying a similar understanding, I told myself, "All right, you feel you're going to die if you step onto this bridge, and you think this feeling is true. The feelings and thoughts are powerful, but are the feelings and thoughts valid? Look at all those people walking back and forth along the bridge. Maybe they're nervous, maybe they're scared, but they're doing it anyway. So I'm going to try crossing the bridge even though I'm scared."

I stepped for a third time onto the bridge, and even though I was afraid, I kept going—taking small, tentative steps, acknowledging the fear and letting it come up within an open, comforting embrace instead of trying to push it away. With each step I gained more confidence. The tight knot of physical sensations, emotions, and thoughts began to loosen. By the time I reached the middle of the bridge, I saw the building on the other side glowing more brightly. The people crossing back and forth across the bridge also shone with a beautiful intensity from the light pouring in through the bridge. I even felt myself glowing.

Below me, meanwhile, I could see people walking along the streets in comparative darkness. I wondered, "Have they ever felt this lightness, this light?"

This shift in perspective helped me to understand more deeply not only how patterns work but also how we can learn to work with our patterns. One of the great obstacles we face in life is our tendency to surrender very quickly to various knots of thought, feeling, and physical sensation, accepting them as truths that keep us from taking the first step onto our own bridge.

Each of us has our own set of patterns, our own bridges to cross. Some of us are stuck in habitual ways of seeing ourselves as vulnerable, incompetent, lonely, unlovable, stressed, or tired. Some of us see others as threats or competitors. Some react adversely to circumstances as varied as traffic jams or weather conditions. Some of us see ourselves through the lens of chronic illness or physical or emotional abuse.

I don't diminish for one moment any of the responses we face when we arrive at a particular bridge and are frozen by a particular pattern that prevents us from stepping across. I only want to point out that it's possible, after recoiling from the first step, to pause for a moment, examine our thoughts, feelings, and sensations, and ask ourselves whether or not the things we accept as fact are true.

REAL BUT NOT TRUE

The fear I felt was real—in the sense that I was fully experiencing it—but it wasn't based on true circumstances. Rather, it was triggered by residual memories of past experiences of falling from great heights and feeling pain and by misperceptions of the immediate circumstances. The bridge was so obviously solid, and the fear I felt about crossing it didn't take into account the truth that so many people were moving back and forth across it without falling through. .

So I had to engage in a little conversation with myself: "Yes, what you're feeling is real. I recognize and honor that. But this fear is not based on true conditions." At some point as I was wrestling with this experience a kind of mantra occurred to me. *Mantra* is a Sanskrit term, usually understood as a special combination of ancient syllables that form a sort of prayer or invocation that help to open our being to a deeper connection to possibilities beyond our immediate conceptualization. In my own small case of trying to cross a bridge there were no mysterious syllables, only four simple words: *Real but not true.*

Repetition of this mantra has become a practice for me: a recognition that when I feel troubled in any way, the feelings of a particular challenge are real in terms of thought and feeling. But however strongly such thoughts and feelings may arise, they're not based on immediate circumstances. I began to see that the challenge of crossing the bridge was actually an opportunity to educate the part of myself that identified with and as a pattern of fear.

A mantra is basically a means of talking with your thoughts and feelings. It's a time-honored method sometimes referred to as prayer, but really it's an opening of a conversation between the heart and the mind.

I invite you now to participate in a little mantra exercise when faced with challenges, whether that means crossing a glass bridge; being stuck in traffic and being late for work or a meeting; dealing with a coworker, a manager, your spouse, partner, or children; or talking with bank officials.

Take a nice, deep breath, observing your inhalation and exhalation.

Then take a moment to greet your feelings as guests. Say "Hello," and start a conversation. You can begin by saying something like "Yes, I know that you're real."

Then ask "Are you true? Are you based on present conditions, or are you based on past experiences?"

Ask yourself again and again if what you're experiencing is real or true, until mentally and emotionally you can accept your feelings as real but the conditions on which they're based as possibly not true. Such momentary pauses can transform your understanding of who you are and what you're capable of—and in the same instant encourage others to step onto their own bridges and experience the same lightness.

This book is about crossing bridges. It's about taking pauses that enable us approach patterns of fear, resentment, jealousy, grief, and rage with gentleness and respect. It's about taking a moment to remember the truth about who we truly are and to remind ourselves to be kind to ourselves when we get caught up in our patterns and to be gentle with others when they get caught up in theirs.

WHEN PATTERNS COLLIDE

It's also about building bridges. When we begin to recognize and work with our own patterns, a subtle yet momentous chain of events begins to evolve. We begin to develop a more open and compassionate response toward family members, friends, coworkers, and others who are entwined in our personal lives. We begin to recognize and experience a "kindness" toward them; a realization that, "Hey, so-and-so is a lot like me! He (or she) has fears, needs, desires, and frustrations, just like I do."

From that simple recognition, we can begin to transform our view of ourselves and others in a positive way.

To use a small example, while in London recently I was wandering through a small shop when I heard a lot of screaming outside. I stepped out of the shop and saw a woman standing in the street in an open space next to the curb, while her two children stood terrified on the sidewalk.

A man was slowly pulling up to the space to park his car and the woman was shouting, "Stop! Stop! You can't park here!"

The louder she screamed, the closer he came.

From his open window, he said, "If you stop screaming, I'll go."

But she kept on screaming.

So he came closer. I thought he might actually run her over, or, since he was going so slowly, she might reach into his window and try to hit him.

Again, he said, "Lady, stop screaming. What's your problem?"

But she didn't stop, and he pulled in closer, until his car was almost on top of her.

Finally he came so close, she stopped screaming. After taking a couple of deep breaths, she explained, "Look, my husband has been looking for hours for a place to park. I found this spot and I've stood here protecting it until he drove down this street again."

The driver replied, "Lady, if you'd said that from the beginning instead of just screaming at me, I would have moved on. But you didn't give me a chance to understand what was going on. Please, just watch your reactions in the future." And a moment later he mumbled, "And I guess I'll watch mine."

Then he drove off, giving a little wave to the woman and her children huddling on the street.

The woman stepped back from the street and hugged her children, murmuring, "I'm sorry. That was bad. I'm a bad momma."

I felt as though I ought to go up to her and say she wasn't bad—any more than the man driving the car was bad. Both of them were simply surrendering to patterns. She was caught up in the belief that the guy in the car was trying to steal something from her and reacted blindly out of that belief. But the guy in the car didn't know what was going on. All he saw was someone screaming at him, attacking him verbally—and that triggered a pattern in him, perhaps defensive, which raised his anger at being yelled at. So one pattern was fighting the other.

But approaching her at that time, in that place, would not have been appropriate. Can you imagine going through an experience like that and having some short, bald stranger walk up to you and try to explain Buddhist teachings in a phrase or two?

Besides, I think she learned a bit about patterns from that encounter and didn't need me to explain the lesson to her. Neither she nor the guy in the car may have described their interaction in terms of patterns, but it seemed apparent that they both came to a realization that they were being led blindly by *something* toward a confrontation that could have turned quite ugly—and at the last moment turned away from it.

Such situations, in which patterns collide, occur all too often. Unfortunately, unless we've had some training in looking at and working with our patterns—the type of training offered in the following pages—we don't recognize when we're in their grip. (Even when we *do* have some training we don't always recognize what's happening—as in my own experience at the edge of the glass bridge.) In such cases, the parties involved don't step back to look at the patterns driving them, and arguments can escalate, resulting in long-standing grudges, interpersonal violence, and, on a larger scale, war.

I'd like to think that the reason these two people backed away from a potentially violent situation was because they both saw the children huddling in terror on the sidewalk. As a father myself, I am a bit sensitive to the needs of children, to their fears and nightmares, their longings, and the pressures that their friends and the cultures within which they're raised exert upon them. After my daughters were born, each time I held their small bodies in my arms—listening to their breath, watching their eyes move back and forth, seeing them smile—I was reminded of one of the most basic of the Buddha's teachings: that all life is precious and that protecting and preserving life is our most important responsibility.

OPEN HEART, OPEN MIND

A large part of that responsibility involves developing a deeper understanding of the patterns that drive our thoughts, feelings, and behaviors so that we don't surrender to the impulse to blindly follow them. As we begin to comprehend the ways in which our own experiences and the lessons of the cultures in which we've been raised have shaped the ways in which we view ourselves and the world around us, we begin to open up to the possibility that so many of the misunderstandings that arise between individuals, communities, and nations stem from a stubborn clinging to patterns, to beliefs that what we think and feel is "right" and that what others think and feel is "wrong."

Once we begin to open our hearts to the possibility that a situation is a little bit less certain than we initially supposed, we can begin to open our minds toward those whose behavior is abusive or antagonistic. We cross a bridge. We begin to wonder why people don't see the same light, and we develop a desire to help them. The desire to help others, the desire to build relationships begins to grow. We start to see others' patterns, and as we do so we begin to understand people a little differently. We even begin to feel some sympathy toward them. We find ourselves more and more willing and able to engage—to say, in our own way, "Stop screaming." We give them a chance to explain their behaviors, their beliefs. And in that moment, we offer ourselves and someone else a chance to open up in unexpected ways.

AN UNUSUAL GIFT

Several years ago, shortly after the September 11 attacks, an American friend of mine was spending Christmas in Paris. As he was walking down the street on Christmas Day, he was stopped by someone who appeared to be of Middle Eastern descent, who asked him, "Are you American?"

My friend was confronted by a choice: walk away from a potentially violent confrontation as quickly as possible, or answer the question. His fear-based pattern urged him to walk away, but he chose to let the urge remain in the background—to see it as a bridge to cross.

"Yes," he answered, "I'm an American."

He waited a couple of moments for an attack.

None came.

Instead, the man confronting him said, "I want to apologize on behalf of my people for the attack on your country. We don't all hate you, and we're sorry for what happened. I understand if you hate me, but I beg you not to hate me or my people."

Taken aback by what he initially considered a threat, my American friend just said, "Thank you."

Later he would say that it was the most unusual Christmas present he'd ever received. This stranger gave him the gift of his own humanity, which was quite precious. At the same time, the exchange exposed some of the darker areas of his own personality—bigotry, fear, and suspicion—and offered him the opportunity to examine them more deeply and determine whether his reactions were real or true.

Interactions such as this one and the exchange between the woman and the driver in London represent the possibility that we can cross bridges and develop relationships that gather a kind of positive momentum, which, passed from one person to another, can ultimately awaken us one by one and enable us to impact people in our lives, communities, and nations. The insights and practices offered in the following pages present a way of looking at ourselves and the world around us a bit more generously. It offers a means of crossing bridges, building new ones, and repairing old ones.

These are all steps in a long journey, one that I hope for each of you who read this will last a lifetime.

TWO

Starting Out

My own journey began when, at eight years old, I overheard a tense, whispered discussion between my mother and grandfather in the kitchen of our small house in a quiet little village in northern Nepal. A letter had been sent to my father from the Sixteenth Karmapa, the head of one of the four principal spiritual orders of Tibetan Buddhism. For those of you who may be unfamiliar with Tibetan Buddhism in particular—or Buddhism in general—a little explanation may be necessary to understand why this letter, from this man, changed my life.

LINEAGE

In the years after the Buddha passed away, his teachings began spreading to many countries across Asia. After many centuries, they were carried to Tibet, a country whose geographic isolation offered an ideal setting for successive generations of students and teachers to devote themselves exclusively to study and practice. Those who had achieved some mastery would then pass what they'd learned to their most capable students—who, in their turn, passed what they'd learned and experienced to their own students. In this way, unbroken lineages of teaching were established in Tibet.

There are currently four major lineages, also known as schools, of Tibetan Buddhism: Nyingma, Sakya, Kagyu, and Gelug. Each of these major schools developed at different times and in different areas of Tibet. They share the same basic principles, practices, and beliefs; the differences among them lie mainly in their approaches to learning and practice. The oldest of these schools is known as the Nyingma—a Tibetan term that may be roughly translated as "the older ones."

The emergence of Buddhism in Tibet can be traced back to the seventh century C.E., a period when Tibet was a unified country ruled by an emperor. According to the historical records that remain to us, an emperor by the name of Songtsen Gampo married a Chinese princess, who brought with her not only her Buddhist convictions but also an impressive statue of the Buddha. It appears that she quickly converted the emperor and many influential people in his court to Buddhism from the native spiritual practice known as Bön. It is also said that Songtsen Gampo married a second wife, a Nepalese princess who was also a Buddhist. These were, as I understand history, political marriages, intended to cement relations between rulers of different countries.

The immediate heirs of Songtsen Gampo, however, were less than enthused about Buddhism and were apparently torn between their allegiance to their native religion and the convictions promoted by Songtsen Gampo and influential members of the court.

However, one of his descendants, King Trisong Detsen—who ruled Tibet during the latter half of the eighth century C.E.—established Buddhism as the official state religion and invited several renowned

Buddhist teachers to Tibet. Among them was a very powerful master named Padmasabhava, often referred to as Guru Rinpoche, a term which means "precious teacher." He spent more than half a century in Tibet, teaching and performing tremendous miracles, such as averting earthquakes. He is also said to have hidden thousands of teachings, known in Tibetan as *termas*, or treasures, which would be discovered in later centuries, during times of great need, by reincarnations of his principal disciples, who would become known as *tertöns*, or treasure finders.

During King Trisong Detsen's rule, the first Buddhist monastery in Tibet was built and several Tibetans were ordained as monastics and charged with overseeing the translation of Buddhist writings from Sanskrit into Tibetan. These teachers and their students are widely considered the founders of the Nyingma school, the first generation of people who translated and codified the teachings of the Buddha in the mountains of Tibet.

Resistance to Buddhist beliefs and practices continued for many years. The last of the Tibetan emperors, Langdarma, assassinated his predecessor and began a brutal repression of Buddhism. Four years into his reign, Langdarma was himself assassinated.

For nearly two centuries after Langdarma's death, the Nyingma lineage of Buddhist teachings remained a kind of "underground" movement, as Tibet underwent enormous political changes, eventually reforming itself into a series of separate but loosely federated feudal kingdoms.

These political changes, however, eventually provided an opportunity for Buddhism to slowly and quietly reassert its influence, as Indian teachers traveled to Tibet and Tibetan students made the difficult journey across the Himalayas to study directly under Indian Buddhist masters.

Among the first schools to take root in Tibet during this period was the Kagyu lineage, which takes its name from the Tibetan terms *ka*, roughly translated into English as "speech" or "instruction," and *gyu*, a Tibetan term that basically means "lineage," in the sense of an unbroken line. The basis of the Kagyu school lies in the tradition of "whispering," or privately speaking, teachings from master to student, preserving in this way a unique purity of transmission.

There's no equivalent in Western culture for this kind of direct and continuous transmission. The closest we can come to imagining how it might work is to think of someone like Albert Einstein approaching his most able students and saying, "Excuse me, but I'm now going to dump everything I've ever learned into your brain. You keep it for a while, and if I come back in another body twenty or thirty years from now, you can dump everything I've taught you back into the brain of some youngster you'll only be able to recognize as me through the insights I'm passing on to you. Oh, and by the way, I may not return—or perhaps not in a form or a manner you'll recognize—so you'll need to pass everything I'm now going to teach you to a few other students whose qualities you'll be able to recognize on the basis of what I'm about to show you—just to make sure that nothing gets lost."

The Kagyu tradition originated in India during the tenth century C.E., when an extraordinary man named Tilopa awoke to his full potential. Over several generations, his insights and the practices through which he achieved them were passed from master to student around Asia, eventually reaching Tibet. The Kagyu lineage of Tibetan Buddhism descends through a man called Marpa, who made three arduous treks across the Himalayas in order to gather teachings from Naropa, the principal student of Tilopa.

Marpa passed these teachings to a young man by the name of Milarepa, who is widely regarded as the "patron saint" of Tibet. Wandering through mountains and valleys, he lived in caves, often teaching through songs and poems. Milarepa, in turn, transmitted everything he'd learned to two of his most promising students, Gampopa and Rechungpa, who established their own schools in different areas of Tibet.

Gampopa and Rechungpa were respectively considered the "sun" and "moon" of the whispered teachings of the Kagyu lineage. Gampopa taught far and wide, attracting many students; hence, he and his teachings were said to "shine like the sun." Rechungpa's following was smaller, his teachings more secret; and like Guru Rinpoche before him, he hid many of his most precious teachings for future generations—perhaps foreseeing that the small and select group of his direct lineage holders would diminish over time and his lineage would eventually vanish.

Over the centuries, the major schools often diverged into small sub-schools. Such a development isn't so hard to understand if you can imagine a land divided by numerous mountains and valleys, rather loosely connected by goat and other animal paths, which made travel and communication rather challenging—even during the few short warm months that break up a long and arduous winter season, when snowfall can reach above a man's head and the temperature drops well below zero. The teachers in these secluded regions, while never deviating from the core Buddhist principles, developed slightly different teachings and practices.

One of these sub-schools is known as the Drukpa Kagyu school. *Drukpa* is the Tibetan word for "dragon," a type of being that in many cultures is considered very old and very wise. The whispers of the dragon—the teachings of the Drukpa Kagyu—are quite precious. The founder of the school, Drogon Tsangpa Gyare Yeshe Dorje, was a student of a *tertön* named Ling Rengpa, who discovered some of the most important *termas* hidden by Rechungpa, which were eventually absorbed into the Drukpa Kagyu school.

That's a *short* version of the history of Tibetan Buddhism!

Imagine the despair of a teenage boy having to learn the long version. I've forgotten half the names and dates of all the people and events involved—mostly because I wasn't the most conscientious student during my training. And also because, frankly, I'm more interested in passing along the lessons I've learned to the people who need them most.

Many of these lessons were passed down through the Tsoknyi Rinpoche lineage, which had been kept and protected by masters of the Drukpa Kagyu lineage.

So before I could begin to fulfill my role as a teacher, I had to find out who I was supposed to be.

REINCARNATIONS

The first Tsoknyi Rinpoche was born in the mid-nineteenth century and mastered all of the teachings of the Drukpa Kagyu lineage. He also uncovered some unique principles and practices that had been known only by Rechungpa and hidden for a thousand years.

According to tradition, the first Tsoknyi Rinpoche was actually an incarnation of Rechungpa, and also of a great Nyingma master and *tertön*, Ratna Lingpa, who lived in the fifteenth century C.E.

I can't describe exactly how the hiding and the revelation of these treasured teachings work. Nor can I say how different teachers, who lived centuries apart, come together to spread their combined wisdom. I can only say that when great masters achieve a certain level of enlightenment, they can emanate in many forms—perhaps as a piece of music or a cool wind on a hot day. They become a kind of energy that sometimes coalesces as teachers in human form.

According to Tibetan tradition, the first Tsoknyi Rinpoche passed his deepest understandings to his most trusted students, many of whom were members of the Drukpa Kagyu lineage and students of the Nyingma lineage. They, in turn, were charged with passing along the teachings to his next reincarnation, who would pass them to his most trusted students. These students, in turn, would eventually pass them along to the next incarnation, who turned out to be a boy who was much more interested in running around with his friends than in saving the world.

So there you are. One day you're a boy playing games with local children; the next day you're a dragon.

A CHANGE OF VIEW

The letter my father had received from the Sixteenth Karmapa stated that I'd been identified as the third incarnation of Tsoknyi Rinpoche.

Rinpoche is a Tibetan term that may be roughly translated as "precious one," a title appended to the name of a great master, similar to the way *PhD* is appended to the name of someone considered an expert in various branches of academic study. *Tsoknyi* is a combination term. *Tsok* is broadly understood to mean "accumulation," and *nyi* is the Tibetan word for the number two. In the Tibetan Buddhist tradition, *tsoknyi* refers to the accumulation of two qualities believed necessary for a person to progress, not only along his or her own path but—far more important—to advance to the point of being able to help others break through their own patterns. These two qualities are known, respectively, as *merit*, a type of momentum accumulated when performing actions that benefit others, and *wisdom*, also known as *insight* into the true nature of existence.

Though I do my best, I can't really say that I measure up to the accomplishments of the men who previously held the title. In addition to being an extraordinary scholar who mastered the finer points of two different schools, or lineages, of Tibetan Buddhism, the first Tsoknyi Rinpoche was apparently a bit of a rebel. I liked that about him when I learned about his activities. He spent a great deal of time and energy overturning centuries of Tibetan cultural prejudice, initiating a massive program to rebuild nunneries and retreat centers for women in eastern Tibet in order to ensure that they would receive education and training equal to men. He also brought together the teachings of both the Drukpa Kagyu and the Nyingma lineage and the secret lessons revealed by Ratna Lingpa to create a unique lineage, many of the lessons of which I've passed down to my own students.

Before moving on, though, I must speak a little bit about the second Tsoknyi Rinpoche. Born in the early twentieth century into the royal family of Nangchen in eastern Tibet, he carried on both his predecessor's dedication to scholarship and his commitment to educating and empowering women. He perished during the Cultural Revolution, but throughout his life, especially in the years before his capture and detention, he provided a means by which a number of the women who trained in the nunneries and retreat centers he'd maintained were able to survive in hiding for decades, secretly practicing and passing to other women the wisdom they'd gained. Political conditions have changed sufficiently to allow these courageous women to teach and practice more openly, and with the help of many generous donors to begin to rebuild the places of learning and practice for women in Tibet.

One of the greatest of these courageous women, a woman in her mid-eighties, died a few years ago. I mourn her loss and at the same time celebrate her dedication and the insights she developed over the course of forty years in hiding, which, fortunately, she was able to share with younger women.

THE *TULKU* PROBLEM

I knew nothing of such extraordinary commitments as I eavesdropped on the conversation between my mother and grandfather as they discussed the letter from the Sixteenth Karmapa. At eight years old, I was mainly concerned with what all this hushed drama had to do with *me*. I wasn't terribly surprised to overhear that I was the reincarnation of somebody-or-other. In many Asian societies, the idea of reincarnation is accepted as a matter of course, as deeply ingrained as notions of heaven and hell are embedded in other cultures.

At the same time, I'd learned enough about Tibetan Buddhism to understand that being recognized as the incarnation of an important teacher, known in Tibetan as a *tulku*, or "emanation body," is a bit more complicated. A *tulku* is the reincarnation of someone who has dedicated himself, through lifetimes of study and practice, to breaking through mental and emotional habits that nowadays would probably be described as "dysfunctional" in order to help all living beings attain the same freedom.

At eight years old, though, I didn't feel like a *tulku*. I had no memories of previous lives or past teachings. I didn't feel moved to save everyone in the universe. I definitely didn't want to be sent away to a monastery for training, as two of my older brothers, who'd also been identified as *tulkus*, had. I wanted to carry on with the relatively carefree life I'd been leading—playing with my childhood friends, climbing trees and mountains, and daring each other to jump across some of the wide streams that ran in and around our village.

My mother and grandmother often pleaded with me to stop; maybe I was a little bit more careful about climbing too high and took a bit more care about not messing my clothes and shoes. But their pleas didn't really have much effect on my adventurous nature; I just learned to take a little bit more care about how I looked when I got home and—not unlike other children—to answer a bit more vaguely when my mother or grandmother asked me what I'd been doing all day.

There was also a family reputation to consider. My grandfather was a meditation master of great renown in our little corner of Nepal. He was the center of spiritual gravity, not only for our village but for much of the surrounding area. He was also a direct descendant of one of the most distinguished royal families of Tibet. And here I was, an eight-year-old boy running around with village kids, climbing cliffs and trees, flirting with girls, and generally making a mess of my family's reputation.

My family lived quite modestly, though, and my mother and grandmother were more concerned about my safety than any other consequences. And in spite of their anxieties, they allowed me a lot of freedom. Perhaps they recognized that I was something of an independent child and would probably just do what I wanted anyway, regardless of their warnings. The most they hoped for was to instill in me a little sense of caution—a plea to avoid taking too many risks.

When I was finally sent to Tashi Jong monastery for training at the age of twelve—four years after my father had received the letter of identification—those early years of freedom both strained and saved my life. I found myself in a situation that was far more structured than the carefree style I'd enjoyed before. Though I tried to adapt to an intense regimen of study and a long set of rules and regulations about "proper" *tulku* behavior, the independent-minded child in me rebelled. I found myself shifting back and forth between trying to be a model student and resenting the rules.

My rebellion began slowly. I started socializing with young people from the surrounding villages, including groups that included girls—a scandalous activity that caused some gossip. Sometimes I encouraged some of my fellow students to sneak out of the monastery to a house in the nearby village, where, for a small fee, people could watch kung fu movies (of which I'm still a fan) on a small black-and-white television set.

After four years, however, the conflict between my longing for freedom and the demands of my training became so intense that I began to speak about the problem to some of my teachers. To my surprise, they didn't order me to conform to discipline. Instead they told me that I wasn't the first person to experience a struggle between established rules and a deep longing for freedom, and I probably wouldn't be the last. They told me that there was a source within me that was very powerful, but in order to access it, I needed to learn a few things about what the Buddha taught.

BALANCE

The Buddha himself, they said, had tried to follow the teachings of masters of other traditions. Dissatisfied with what he'd learned, he went his own way and discovered a fresh view of the patterns that contribute to the pain, sorrow, and dissatisfaction we often feel as we move through life. More important, he discovered the means by which we can reach back through those patterns and reconnect with the openness and warmth we once experienced as very young children but which for many of us, sadly, remains a distant memory.

My teachers urged me to find a balance between the training I'd received to fulfill my role as a *tulku* and the promptings of my heart. Through their encouragement and assistance, I was able to complete my training. In the process, however, I learned something quite startling: The youthful freedom I longed for was no different than the freedom of heart that the Buddha and the teachers who have followed in his footsteps had taught. The discipline of my training was aimed at helping people understand and work with their patterns, to embrace them with the same warmth, openness, and curiosity with which most of us approached the various phenomena we encountered as very young children.

A HARD CHOICE

Eventually I chose to be released from the monastic vows I'd adopted during the course of my training. It was a slow process, a dawning of a relationship between my heart and my mind, a relationship between the playful freedom of my childhood and the discipline and learning I'd gained during my years at Tashi Jong.

When I was young, I was a very playful person with a lot of energy, with a very bright spark. I had no problem mixing with boys, girls, or older men and women. I enjoyed spending time with them. I was especially appreciative of the ideas and openness to emotion that girls and women appeared to express much more easily than boys and men. But when I arrived at the monastery there were so many rules about the people we could talk to or with whom we could interact. My joy, my spark dimmed for a while. I found the rigid rules of conduct and the strict demands of training oppressive.

Gradually, during my *tulku* training, I grew to accept that, while the teachings themselves are very rich in terms of describing the nature of reality, the basis of being human, and the vital role that compassion plays in awakening our hearts and minds, I found it hard to relate to them except in an intellectual way. Please understand that I'm only speaking for myself. Many people, across centuries and cultures, have discovered—and continue to discover—profound inspiration in the traditional manner of transmission. I'm just not one of them. I understand ideas best when I've worked through them in terms of experience—and particularly in the context of interacting with other people.

Of course, interacting with other people meant interacting with women, who represent a little more than half of the human population. During my visits to the village near Tashi Jong, I found that I wasn't able to resist talking to the girls, flirting with them a little, and listening to their complaints about their position in society. They were intelligent young ladies, well informed about developments in Western cultures. And they were undeniably attractive—all the more so because contact with them was forbidden by the monastic vows that inhibit conversation with women.

At twenty-two years old, after I'd completed my training, I finally summoned the courage to approach someone with a request to relinquish the monastic vows I'd taken when I entered Tashi Jong. Although there are numerous vows of conduct one is required to take as a monk, relinquishing them is actually a simple process. Generally one asks the master from whom one has taken one's vows to be released from them. Since the man from whom I'd taken my vows had passed away by that time, I simply approached another teacher and asked to be released. I still hold to what are generally known as "householder vows"—which include refraining from killing, lying, stealing, overindulgence in intoxicants, and abusive sexual behaviors. But there are deeper vows, including the *bodhisattva* vow, an oath to do whatever we can to help others achieve freedom from pain and suffering, that even a simple householder like me can keep.

It's not unusual for a *tulku*, especially in the Nyingma tradition, to marry and have children. My father, one of the most brilliant teachers of the Nyingma tradition, married several times. If he hadn't, of course, I would never been born, and you would not be reading this book.

The tradition of what we might call "lay teachers" is, in fact, not uncommon. Marpa, the man who brought the Buddhist teachings to Tibet in the eleventh century C.E., was a married man. Yet we owe the Kagyu tradition to his diligence and dedication. He is known as a "householder" teacher, a man who maintained his commitment even while raising a family and running a large farm.

Of course, many people in the Tibetan Buddhist community were disappointed by my decision to drop my monastic vows. Gossip flourished. "Oh Tsoknyi Rinpoche is such a bad *tulku*." "Tsoknyi Rinpoche is only interested in women." "Tsoknyi Rinpoche doesn't care about anyone but himself." Hearing such gossip was painful. But deep in my heart, I was certain that relinquishing my monastic vows was, for me, the correct choice. Several years after I gave up my vows, I married a woman who is far more intuitive and intelligent than I could ever hope to be. We've spent the last two decades working out many of the same issues that other married couples deal with and have worked together in raising two daughters. My experience as a married man and a father has offered me the opportunity to develop a greater sensitivity to the issues faced by household practitioners across the world.

AN ACCIDENTAL TEACHER

Between my decision to drop my vows and my marriage, I accidentally became a teacher.

It happened this way. Many great teachers understood my reasons and continued to accept me as a student. Shortly after I'd dropped my monastic vows, I traveled to Bodhgaya, India—the place where the Buddha had achieved enlightenment—to receive teachings from Dilgo Khyentse Rinpoche, the head of the Nyingma school of Tibetan Buddhism until his passing in 1991. Graciously, Rinpoche appointed me as his subordinate teacher; that is, he would teach for a short while on essential points, lead the group in a bit of meditation practice, and depart—directing me to explain his teachings. I took this appointment as a kind of trust. He gave me the opportunity to expand on a ten-minute teaching for a lesson that sometimes consumed three hours.

Afterward I would take a walk to the area of Bodhgaya where the Buddha is said to have attained enlightenment while meditating under a tree that is now often called the Bodhi tree (*bodhi* being a Sanskrit and a Pali term that is usually translated as "awakened"). Many temples and shrines have been built in that place—which also contains a descendant of the original Bodhi tree.

As I wandered among these places, I was approached by a person I had met a few years before at Tashi Jong.

"Would you be willing to talk privately to us a little but more about what Dilgo Khyentse Rinpoche was saying?" he asked.

"Of course," I replied.

The next day about ten people showed up in the small room I occupied in a nearby Tibetan Buddhist monastery.

The day after that, thirty people showed up.

The day after that, more than a hundred people showed up, cramming the room and the hallways.

I'm not sure what attracted so many people. Dilgo Khyentse Rinpoche was one of the most brilliant teachers the twentieth century has ever seen. Maybe behind the scenes he encouraged people to come to me. Maybe some people were attracted by the fact that I was a *tulku* who had renounced monastic vows to lend whatever little wisdom I'd gained to people who were living householder lives—married men and women who were trying to reconcile Buddhist philosophy and practice with the task of holding down a job, maintaining a personal relationship, or raising a family.

Eventually the crowds became so large that it was necessary to rent a hall in one of the local monasteries to accommodate all the people who wanted to hear from a person who was the subject of much gossip and disgrace.

Shortly after I returned to Nepal from Bodhgaya, I received an invitation from one of the people who had attended my teachings to teach in Argentina. I spent a couple of months there teaching—but also meeting, conversing, and sharing meals with wonderful, caring, openhearted people. Following that teaching I was invited to North America, Malaysia, and other countries.

Especially after I dropped my vows, I never dreamed that I would become someone who spends most months out of the year traveling to different places. I was quite content with living a rather quiet life, marrying, raising children, and dealing with everyday problems of paying bills.

Of course, I'd never expected as a child to be identified as the reincarnation of a Buddhist teacher, either.

Life takes such interesting turns, which on the surface can seem, to put it mildly, unpleasant. But one thing I've learned is that you never know where these turns are going to take you. One day you're a child with no greater interests than playing games and climbing trees. The next day you're a reincarnation of a legendary master. Later you're a disgraced monk, and a few years after that, you're a worldwide teacher.

Anything is possible. The point is to keep your heart and mind open to the likelihood of change—a subject that will be discussed as we go along through the following pages.

I owe as much to my family and the friends I've met around the world during my teaching career as I do to the great teachers under whom I've trained. Each, in their own way, has helped me to advance a step or two across any number of bridges. They've helped me to treat my own and others' patterns with kindness and clarity. They've helped me to understand that the essence of the Buddha's teachings was aimed at helping us to become fully and healthily human, and they have, in their own ways, contributed to my learning how to interpret these teachings in a way that is relevant to contemporary society.

SKILLFULNESS

Many of us tend to think of ourselves as busy, bored, frustrated, unhappy, tired, sick, or poor; burdened by questions about how we can feed our children, pay our mortgages, our rent, and other bills. These are valid considerations. I only want to point out that there's a different way of looking at our situations, that there's a different way of looking at who we are and what we're capable of achieving.

Of course, adopting a shift in perspective involves effort. There are no shortcuts, no secrets to developing a fresh, enlivening, and uplifting understanding of ourselves and the circumstances surrounding our lives. It's taken a long time for each of us to build up the patterns that contribute to an image of ourselves as limited, wounded, or helpless, and it's going to take a long time and a good deal of work to break through such images.

Some may question whether the possibility of transforming our perspective is worth the work involved. After more than twenty years of teaching around the world and speaking with thousands of people, it's become clear to me that for many of us it's more comfortable living with what we know, even it's painful. To venture off into the realm of the unfamiliar—to let go of entrenched habits of thought, feeling, and perception—is just too hard to imagine. Who wants to give up the comfort of familiarity, especially when the price of doing so requires looking at ourselves and the way we live our lives with courage, intelligence, and ingenuity? It's much easier to conform to the social and cultural habits ingrained in us from an early age, to attempt to improve our inner lives by making changes to our outer lives.

The sort of "looking" that the Buddha encouraged didn't necessarily involve making a long list of our mistakes or faults or settling back into some quietly composed mental and emotional state to contemplate the nature of the universe. Since many of the people he taught were laborers and craftspeople, the word he used to characterize this sort of examination was one to which they could easily relate: skillfulness. It requires a certain combination of commitment, intelligence, and practice to develop the kind of skill required to plant a field, tend crops, harvest them, and bring them to market; to create a vessel from a lump of raw clay; to spin; to weave; to work metal or wood.

The same skillfulness they applied to their work, the Buddha taught, could also be applied to their thoughts, emotions, and behavior. In other words, people could, by deepening their understanding of their basic nature and following certain practices, become more skillful at being human.

Through a combination of intelligent inquiry, dedication, and practical experience, we can uncover the various patterns that have ruled our lives for many years. We can sort through our experiences and begin to distinguish between life lessons that are useful and the residue of fear, competitiveness, anger, frustration, and so on that we've accumulated along the way.

THE SANDWICH PROBLEM

A young lady who'd been hired to fill an executive role in a marketing firm recently expressed some frustration with her job and with the behavior of her immediate superior.

"Is this the job that was described to me?" she said. "No. Is my boss a little crazy? Probably. For him, everything—and I mean *everything*—is a fire that has to be put out before it spreads. I can understand that certain types of publicity can produce a negative view of the company, but they're not going to cost any lives.

"In my previous job, the atmosphere was a little bit more mellow. I was launching a product, and we took a slow and steady approach to launching it. In this job, I have to deal with launching something under a person who sees everything as a crisis and often interrupts whatever work I'm doing. He also thinks I want his job, which I don't. Do I want this job? Of course. There are many people—my family, my friends, my coworkers—who depend on me. Do I like the craziness from above? No. But after a few months here, I've learned that the conditions aren't going to change, so I have to adjust my attitude, finding the right balance between fulfilling my obligations while dealing with a crazy boss and people who depend on me to help them keep their jobs, and the people who are going to receive a product that may be useful to them."

I call the issue that this woman is going through a "sandwich problem." She's the cheese and tomato caught between two slices of bread pressing in on her from both sides. I began to notice the sandwich problem first in the Asian countries in which I teach, where many people seemed to be caught in the middle of relationships between their wives and their mothers, both of whom vie for control of the family home. Ordinarily the husband defers to his mother, as the elder; but some wives, especially in the younger generation, are challenging their mother-in-law's traditionally absolute rule. The guy in between is challenged by both sides of the sandwich. He has to accept that sometimes there may be no solution to the problem and that no solution is the solution. He can't take sides. He has to let each side, each slice of bread, come to a resolution on its own.

This may seem at first like resignation, but actually it's a quite skill-ful means of allowing people on different sides of a dispute to settle it themselves.

VIRTUOSITY

Over many years, scholars and translators have linked the Buddha's teachings about skillfulness with the concept of living what is often described as "virtuous life"—an idea that strikes a chord of anxiety into the hearts of people new to Buddhism (and quite a few long-term practitioners). Recently I heard that someone who'd attended a teach-ing that included some discussion of virtue whispered to someone next to him, "Does this mean I have to erase the rap songs from my iPod?"

I don't know whether or not the exchange actually occurred, or with those exact words. But hearing about it, given my own checkered history, afforded me one of the biggest belly laughs I've enjoyed in a long time.

The subject of virtue has been debated and defined in various ways by different schools of Buddhism—as well as other religious and philo-sophical traditions—over the centuries. Scholars and translators have added their own voices to the discussion. There are many stories about

Buddhist monastics who, in the centuries following the Buddha's passing, took exceptional precautions to avoid stepping on insects or the possibility of inhaling them.

So it's quite natural that people might wonder what virtue means in the context of modern life, with its abundance of choices and challenges. At various times, people have asked, "Do I have to become a vegetarian?" "Do I have to give up sex, alcohol, or good food?" "Do I have to stop watching TV?" "Do I have to stop going out with my friends?"

Of course, there's a lot to be said for living simply. Fewer distractions allow us more time to devote to examining our lives and the effects of our thoughts, feelings, and behavior, not only on our own lives but on the lives of all the people with whom we come into contact. But that is only one aspect of skillful living that might be described as virtuous.

In a broad sense, virtue, or virtuous living—as I understand it— comes very close to the Hippocratic oath that doctors take: First, do no harm. The earliest and most persistent descriptions of virtue involve avoiding activities that cause harm to others, including killing, theft, sexual abuse, lying, slander, and gossip. Interestingly enough, they also include activities that may harm oneself, such as overindulging in intoxicants, food, and certain types of habitual activity—understandings that evolved long before terms like "addiction" or "obesity" were defined by modern medicine.

But the Tibetan word *gewa*, which is often translated as "virtue," has a deeper, more significant meaning. Like the old Middle English word *virtue*, which was related to the effectiveness of an herb or other plant to strengthen certain qualities inherent in the body and the mind, *gewa* means making choices that extend our emotional and intellectual strength, illuminate our potential greatness, build our confidence, and enhance our ability to assist those in need of help.

For example, a few years ago, a student told me about the efforts she took to spend time with her elderly mother, who had become ill but refused to be moved from her apartment to a care facility. Although she had a high-pressure job in New York City, this woman took time out every couple of weeks to visit her mother, spend time with her, and even, as she described it, "sit in the living room and watch awful sitcoms, which I hated, but made my mother laugh. I sat through them because I just loved to see her laugh. Some little piece of my heart seemed to feel lighter, or stronger, or bigger when I heard her laugh, despite the fact that she was in such pain."

As the months passed and her mother's condition worsened, she had to arrange for home health care. But during the times she visited, she took on those duties, bathing her, clothing her, settling her in bed. "Sure, it was hard," she said. "But one night I realized that these were the same kinds of things she did for me when I was a child. Something shifted then. Even though I knew my mother was getting worse, a great burden of sadness lifted from me as I began to see the remaining time I had with her as an opportunity to give back what I'd been given."

After her mother's passing, she found herself taking a more active interest in the elderly neighbors in her apartment building, chatting and visiting with them, and sharing the occasional meal. "It became a sort of positive addiction," she explained. "I realized I had not just these skills but a deep desire to be helpful."

Those skills and that desire have extended to her relationships with her coworkers. "I don't like to overstep professional boundaries," she said, "but if I see someone having a bad day or struggling with a project, I'm more apt to ask if everything's okay or if there's anything I can do to help. Mostly I've found that the people I work with just want to vent a little bit. They want someone to listen to them. And I'm happy to do that, because it feels like I'm participating a bit more in life as a whole instead of just focusing on my own career, my own goals. I feel more and more like we're all in this life together—that there's a purpose greater than meeting revenue goals."

A third, and final, understanding of virtue has come from conversations with a few friends and students around the world. Artists who exhibit extraordinary skill in their respective fields are known as "virtuosos"—an English word that comes from an Italian term signifying someone who demonstrates exceptional skill.

"Virtuoso" may not have been a common term in the language the Buddha spoke or in the languages in which his teachings were passed down orally from teacher to student for several hundred years until they were finally written down. However, everything I've learned from my own studies, the teachings I've received, and my own experience as a teacher, counselor, husband, and father suggests to me that what the Buddha discovered during the days and nights he spent meditating under a tree in Bodhgaya, India, was a method through which we can all become virtuosos in the art of living. Each of us is gifted with the ability to recognize within ourselves an astonishing capacity for brilliance, kindness, generosity, and courage. We also have the potential to awaken everyone with whom we come in contact to the possibility of greatness. We become virtuosos to the extent that we develop our potential to the point at which—even without our conscious intention—our actions and our words serve to awaken the "human artist" in everyone.

But in order to do that, we have to understand the basic material with which we're working. A skillful potter has to learn to recognize the qualities and characteristics of a lump of clay with which he or she works. A virtuoso farmer has to understand the relationship between soil and seeds, fertilizer and water, and implement that understanding in terms of actions.

. Likewise, in order to become virtuoso human beings, we have to begin by understanding our basic nature—the clay, so to speak, with which we're given to work.

And that, to me, is the essence of the Buddha's teaching. It's within our power to become virtuoso humans. The process involves a step-by-step examination of the ways in which we relate to ourselves and the world around us. As we integrate this examination into our daily lives, we begin to realize the possibility of living each moment of our lives with a previously unimagined richness and delight. This approach, advanced twenty-five hundred years ago, asks us to look at who we are in terms beyond the stories we tell ourselves about ourselves, about others, and about the world around us.

Who are we? What are we? How can we learn not just to survive but to *thrive* in the midst of the challenges we face moment by moment, day by day, year by year?

These are the basic questions that generations of religious teachers, scholars, philosophers, and scientists have sought to solve.

The answers may surprise you.

THREE

The Spark

As a very young child I used to sit on my grandfather's lap while he meditated. At two or three years old, of course, I had no idea what meditation involved. My grandfather didn't give me instructions and didn't speak to me about his own experience. Yet as I sat with him I felt a sense of deep comfort, together with a kind of childlike fascination with whatever was going on inside and around me. I felt myself becoming aware of *something* growing brighter and more intense in my own body, my own mind, my own heart.

That *something*, when I was old enough to fit words to it, is a kind of spark that lights the lives of all living beings. It has been given various names by people of many different disciplines, and its nature has been debated for centuries. In many Buddhist teachings, it's known as "buddha nature." Don't worry! That doesn't mean that you're meant to walk around in robes, begging for food while wandering the countryside teaching people. Actually the term is a very rough translation of two Sanskrit words, often used interchangeably: *sugatagarbha* or *tathagatagarbha*. *Sugata* may be roughly understood as "gone to bliss," while *tathagata* is usually interpreted as "thus-gone." Both refer to those, like the Buddha, who have transcended or "gone beyond" conflict, delusion,

41

or suffering of any kind—a condition one might reasonably understand as "blissful." *Garbha* is most commonly translated as "essence," although on a subtle level, it may also suggest "seed" or "root." So a more accurate translation of "buddha nature" might be the essence of one who has gone beyond conflict, delusion, and so on to an experience of unclouded bliss. One of the core teachings of Buddhism is that we all possess this essence, this root or seed.

Buddha nature is hard to describe, however, largely because it is limitless. It's a bit difficult to contain the limitless within the sharp boundaries of words and images. Masters of other spiritual traditions have struggled with similar concerns. Even contemporary scientists resist the idea of capturing the physical world in a neat, nice, precise snapshot. Albert Einstein, one of the great scientists of the twentieth century, dismissed the idea of quantum physics—the principles that enable us to go through grocery-market lines with a sweep of a scanner and use mobile-phone applications to contact friends and family members—as "spooky science."

Well, the understanding of Buddha nature may seem a bit spooky to some people, but it's based on more than two thousand years of testing and experience. Although the actual experience of touching our awakened nature defies absolute description, a number of people over the past two millennia have at least tried to illuminate a course of action using words that serve as lights along the way.

EMPTINESS

Traditionally, one of the words that describes the basis of who and what we are—indeed, the basis of all phenomena—has been translated as *emptiness*, a word that, at first glance, might seem a little scary, a suggestion, supported by early translators and interpreters of Buddhist philosophy, that there is some sort of void that permeates our being.

Most of us, at some point in our lives, have experienced some sort of emptiness. We've wondered, "What the am I doing here?" *Here* may be a job, a relationship, a home, a body with creaking joints, a mind with fading memories.

If we look deeper, though, we can see that the void we may experience in our lives is actually a positive prospect.

Emptiness is a rough translation of the Sanskrit term *śūnyatā* and the Tibetan term *tongpa-nyi*. The basic meaning of the Sanskrit word *śūnya* is "zero," an infinitely open space or background that allows for anything to appear. The Tibetan word *tongpa* means "empty"— not in the sense of a vacuum or a void but rather in the sense of the basis of experience that is beyond our ability to perceive with our senses, to describe, to name, or to capture in a nice, tidy concept. Maybe a better understanding of the deep sense of the word may be "inconceivable" or "unnamable." The Sanskrit syllable *ta* and the Tibetan syllable *nyi*, meanwhile, don't necessarily mean anything in themselves, but when added to an adjective or noun, they convey a sense of possibility.

So when Buddhists talk about emptiness as the basis of our being, we don't mean that who or what we are is nothing, a zero or void—a point of view that can give way to a kind of cynicism. For example, there's an old, old story about a man who spent many years in a cave meditating on emptiness. Mice were constantly crawling around his cave, and one day a particularly large one leapt onto the rock that served as his table. "Ha," he thought, "the mouse is emptiness." He grabbed his shoe and killed the mouse, thinking, "The mouse is emptiness, my shoe is emptiness, and killing the mouse is emptiness." But all he'd really done was solidify the idea of emptiness into a concept that nothing exists, so he could do whatever he wanted and feel whatever he felt without experiencing any consequences.

This is a simplistic understanding of emptiness—a point of view that nothing has any meaning. But the actual teachings on emptiness imply an infinitely open space that allows for anything to appear, change, disappear, and reappear. The basic meaning of emptiness, in other words, is "openness" or "potential." At the basic level of our being, we are "empty" of definable characteristics. We aren't defined by our past, our present, or our thoughts and feelings about the future. We have the potential to experience anything. And *anything* can refer to thoughts, feelings, and physical sensations.

To truly understand emptiness, however, it has to be experienced, and in this respect I can offer a story told by a student about how he had, in short order, lost his job, his home, and both of his parents.

"When all this was happening," he said, "I spent a lot of time just looking at the pain, frustration, and sadness I was feeling. As I looked at this great mass of stuff, it came to me that I could break it down into smaller pieces.

"Working with all this pain in this way, I gradually came to experience—not just intellectually but experientially—that *I was not my pain*. That I was not my frustration. Not my sadness. Whoever or whatever I was, I was an observer of my thoughts and feelings and the physical sensations that often accompanied them. Of course I felt some heaviness and wished I could turn time back. But as I looked at what was passing through my mind and body, I realized that there was something bigger than these experiences, something more basic, something that was larger, clearer, and more forgiving than I'd ever experienced. An openness that just let all this stuff come and go without taking it personally or putting it into words, but was felt at the heart of my being. Oh, I'm not explaining this very well. . . ."

Actually, he explained it very well—or as well as he could, since the experience of emptiness doesn't really fit precisely into words. A traditional Buddhist comparison to this experience likens it to giving candy to a mute. The mute can taste the sweetness of the candy but is incapable of describing the taste to anyone else.

But perhaps I can offer a more contemporary example.

MOVIES

Some twenty years ago, I was visiting my oldest brother, Chokyi Nyima Rinpoche, at his monastery in Boudhanath, just outside of Kathmandu. We were sitting together having lunch, laughing and talking, when I noticed a guy sitting at another table staring at me, which made me a little nervous. At one point, Chokyi Nyima Rinpoche left the table and the guy who was staring at me approached. He introduced himself as the director Bernardo Bertolucci, who was in the area making the film *Little Buddha*.

"We're making a movie," he said, "and there is one role that I think you would be perfect for, because I like your smile. Can I come tomorrow with the camera and have you act in front of the camera?"

I said, "Okay."

So the next day he arrived with the cameraman and a camera. The cameraman started shooting and the director asked me to say something and smile. But I found it hard to smile. I'd never smiled into the black hole of a camera lens. I'd only smiled at people while chatting with them.

He asked me to try again, saying I had real potential. "But you have to smile," he said. We tried that a few times, but I didn't really know how to connect whatever small sense of humor I have to a machine. It's always arisen from my contact with people. But Bertolucci wasn't willing to give up. He asked me to come to the set where they were filming to see how movies are made. So I went there for four or five days, and as I watched the whole filming process I became very disillusioned. It all seemed so artificial—all the time it took for makeup, to set up the lights, rehearse a scene over and over again, watching the actors laugh or cry on cue, and then film the scene again and again from different angles.

Watching all this, I thought, "Wow, I thought movies were more real than this."

A couple of days later I had to go to Bhutan, and when I came back I found that they had cast someone else in the role—which I didn't mind so much. I was actually glad not to have to participate in what seemed to me a rather artificial process.

The downside of this experience was that I lost interest in watching movies for four or five years. Every time I watched a scene, I would think, "Oh, they've filmed this scene twenty or thirty times." I couldn't enjoy watching a movie.

Slowly, though, my attitude changed.

"Why shouldn't I like watching movies?" I asked myself. "Life itself is in many ways like a movie. There are lots of causes and conditions that contribute to appearances that create such compelling plots. And the effort that goes into making a movie is similar to the combinations of causes and conditions that come together to create the stuff that we experience in daily life." So now I can watch movies with the same appreciation that I watch life. I can appreciate the beauty of the illusion unfolding. I can appreciate the effort. I can appreciate the story. But I can also maintain a little distance, so that I don't become sucked in.

I can also appreciate the fact that an actor or actress who is shot or stabbed in a movie isn't really dead but is probably sleeping quite comfortably in Los Angeles or working somewhere around the world on another movie. I can still be moved by the story on the screen, but at the same time know it's a movie and that all sorts of things have contributed to making the movie.

We can apply the same sort of understanding to daily life. We can watch our experiences unfold, we can become emotionally and intellectually involved in them, but at the same time recognize that they're a kind of movie.

AN EMPTINESS EXERCISE

I'd like to give you a little taste of emptiness through a practice that has become known as "objectless *shinay.*" *Shinay* is a Tibetan term, a combination of two words: *shi*, which is commonly translated as "calmness" or "peace," and *nay*, which means resting or simply "staying there." In Sanskrit, this practice is known as *shamata*. Like *shi*, *shama* may be understood in a variety of ways, including "peace," "rest," or "cooling down," while *ta*, like *nay*, means to "abide" or "stay." I go back and forth between the Sanskrit and Tibetan terms because, depending on the group of people who come to my teachings, some are more familiar or comfortable with one or the other. The more important point is that, whether in Sanskrit or Tibetan, the term describes a process of cooling down from a state of mental, emotional, or sensory excitement.

Most of us, when we look at something, hear something, or experience a thought or emotion, react almost automatically with some sort of judgment. This judgment can fall into three basic categories: pleasant ("I like this"), unpleasant ("I don't like this"), or confused ("I don't know whether I like this or not"). Each of these categories is often subdivided into smaller categories: pleasant experiences are judged as "good," for example; unpleasant experiences are judged as "bad." As one student expressed it, the confused judgment is just too puzzling ("I usually try to push it out of my mind and focus on something else"). The possibilities represented by all these different responses, however, tempt us to latch on to our judgments and the patterns that underlie them, undermining our attempt to distinguish between real and true.

There are many varieties of *shinay* or *shamata* practice. The one that most closely approaches an experiential rather than a theoretical understanding of emptiness is known commonly as "objectless" because it doesn't involve—as some other variations do—focusing attention on a particular object, like a sound, or a smell, or a physical thing like a flower, a crystal, or a candle flame. Some teachers refer to this practice as "open presence," because it involves being just lightly aware of whatever you're experiencing—internally or externally—right here and now. You're merely present.

The instructions are simple.

Just straighten your spine while keeping the rest of your body relaxed.

Take a couple of deep breaths.

Keep your eyes open—though not so intently that your eyes begin to burn or water. You can blink. But just notice yourself blinking. Each blink is an experience of presence.

Now, let yourself be aware of everything you're experiencing—sights, sounds, physical sensations, thoughts, and emotions. Allow yourself to be open to all these experiences.

Inevitably, as you begin this exercise, all sorts of thoughts, feelings, and sensations will pass through your experience. This is to be expected. This little exercise is in many ways like starting a weight-training program at the gym. At first you can lift only a few pounds for a few repetitions before your muscles get tired. But if you keep at it, gradually you'll find that you can lift heavier weights and perform more repetitions.

Similarly, learning to rest in simple, open presence is a gradual process. At first you might be able to remain open for only a few seconds at a time before thoughts, emotions, and sensations bubble up to the surface and consume your attention. The basic instruction is merely to be aware of everything that passes through your awareness as it is. Whatever you experience, you don't have to suppress it. Even latching on to irritations—"Oh, I wish that person next door would turn down his music" or "I wish the family upstairs would stop yelling at each other"—is part of open presence. Just observe these thoughts and feelings as they come and go—and how quickly they come and go, to be replaced by others. If you keep doing this, you'll get a taste of emptiness—a vast, open space in which possibilities emerge and combine, dance together for a while, and vanish with astonishing rapidity. You'll glimpse one aspect of your basic nature, which is the freedom to experience anything and everything.

Don't criticize or condemn yourself if you find yourself chasing after physical sensations, thoughts, or emotions. No one becomes a buddha overnight. Recognize, instead, that for a few seconds you were able to directly experience something new, something now. You've passed through theory and ventured into the realm of experience. As you begin to let your experiences come and go, we begin to see them as less solid. They may be real, but you begin to question whether they're true.

Experience follows intention. Wherever we are, whatever we do, all we need to do is recognize our thoughts, feelings, and perceptions as something natural. Neither rejecting nor accepting, we simply acknowledge the experience and let it pass. If we keep this up, we'll eventually find ourselves becoming able to manage situations we once found painful, scary, or sad. We'll discover a sense of confidence that isn't rooted in arrogance or pride. We'll realize that we're always sheltered, always safe, and always home.

CLARITY

The exercise just described highlights another aspect of our basic nature, and now I'm going to let you in on a little bit of unconventional
understanding.

As mentioned earlier, according to many standard Tibetan translations, the syllable *nyi* means "ness"—the essential quality of a thing.
But I was taught that the *nyi* of *tongpa-nyi*, on a symbolic level, refers
to *clarity*: the capacity to be aware of all the things we experience, to
see the stuff of our experience and to know that we're seeing it. The
physical and cultural conditions of Tibet have been historically a bit
challenging, so people became masters of developing a shorthand style
of communication that makes today's social media "tweets" seem posi-
tively long-winded. Thus, in the interest of condensed communication,
the Tibetan syllable *nyi* took on a secondary, subtle meaning.

Clarity is the cognizant aspect of our nature: a very simple, basic
capability for awareness. This basic, or natural, awareness is merely a
potential. Just as emptiness is a capacity to *be* anything, clarity is the
capacity to *see* anything. It enables us to recognize and distinguish the
unlimited variety of thoughts, feelings, sensations, and appearances
that continually emerge out of emptiness. Without clarity, we wouldn't
be able to recognize or identify any aspect of our experience. It's not
connected with awareness of any particular *thing*, however. Awareness
of a thing—in terms of a subject (the one who is aware) and an object
(the thing, experience, etc., of which the subject is aware)—is something
we learn as we grow up. The why and the how of that learning process is
a little complex and deserves its own discussion a little later on.

This cognizant, or knowing, aspect of our nature is often described
in Tibetan as *ö-sel-wa*, most commonly translated as "luminosity," a

fundamental capacity to illuminate—or shed light on—our experiences and, thus, to know or be aware of them. In his teachings, the Buddha sometimes compared it to a house in which a lamp has been lit and the shades or shutters have been drawn. The house represents the patterns that bind us to a seemingly solid perspective of ourselves and the world around us. The lamp represents the luminous quality of the spark of our basic nature. No matter how tightly the shades and shutters are closed, inevitably a bit of the light from inside the house shines through. Inside the house, the light from the lamp provides the clarity to distinguish between, say, a chair, a bed, or a carpet—which corresponds to our personal thoughts, feelings, and physical sensations. As this light seeps through the shades or shutters we see other things—people, places, or events. Such experiences may be dualistic; that is to say, reflective of a tendency to perceive experience in terms of "self" and "other," "me" and "not me," but if we take a moment to appreciate such glimpses we can arrive at a deeper, broader experience of basic, or natural, clarity.

Sometimes the challenges we face can produce profound experiences of moments of illumination. That was certainly my experience when trying to cross the glass bridge. Fear compelled me to question my response, which illuminated a pattern, which in turn helped me to see the elements of the pattern in a new light and cross the bridge with a sense of calmness that extended into confidence and, ultimately, a light-heartedness that could be described as joy.

An experience recently described by a young woman offers another, very powerful glimpse into the possibility of transforming obstacles into opportunities.

"I was the youngest child in my family," she explained, "the only girl with two older brothers. My parents gave a lot of attention to them and pinned the hopes of our family on them. I don't blame them for that. That was just part of the culture in which we were raised. Whenever I tried to state an opinion or talk about what I'd learned at school, I was shot down with a remark that what I thought didn't matter. I was just a girl, and a baby, and my only hope in life was to make a good marriage.

"Well, my oldest brother died, and my other brother failed in his business. I did marry a nice man, but he lost his job, so I had to get a job as a secretary in a big business industry.

"But that feeling of not being useful haunted me. I felt I wasn't doing a good enough job or working fast enough, that others in the office were talking behind my back, and that because I wasn't as quick or competent as they were, I would be fired. And if I was fired, how would I support myself and my family? How would I put food on the table? These thoughts and feelings would go on and on until I actually felt myself experiencing the awfulness of living on the street as a beggar.

"I was so terribly afraid.

"The only way I could calm myself down was to look for what I'd heard called a 'light at the end of the tunnel'—a desperate hope that conditions at my job would change, or that I could somehow get another job that paid more. Or maybe I'd get a new boss who didn't demand so much. Or maybe the people whispering behind my back would get fired.

"Then I started looking at my low opinion of myself, and I began to see that the problem wasn't the job but the thoughts and feelings I was having about myself, whether I was in the office or at home trying to make some sort of meal for my husband and two children. Looking for that 'light at the end of the tunnel' was nothing more than the flip side of fear—a hope that some sort of change in circumstances would rescue me from the feeling that I wasn't good enough. Gradually I began to see that hope and fear were nothing more than ideas. They really had nothing to do with my job. They had to do with my thoughts and feelings about my abilities.

"Slowly I began to understand that the light I was looking for was the tunnel and that the tunnel I felt trapped in was the light. The only difference between them was the way I saw myself and my situation. If I saw myself as inadequate, I would perform inadequately. If I saw myself as competent, I would perform competently.

"That clarity has made a huge difference. When I feel incompetent or unimportant, I can look at those thoughts and feelings, and I can see that I have a choice. I can give in to them or I can just look at them. And if I look at them, I learn more about myself and the ability I have to make decisions about how I respond to events in my life."

This woman's story illustrates one of the fundamental principles of the Buddha's teachings. Emptiness and clarity are indivisible. Basically, if you're capable of everything, one of those capabilities is the ability to be aware: to see, to know, or to recognize whatever you're experiencing. You can't separate emptiness from clarity any more than you can separate wetness from water or heat from fire. Your essential nature—your buddha nature—isn't just unlimited in its potential to be; it is also awake and alert to the various forms your experience of life may take.

The key—the how of Buddhist practice—lies in learning to simply rest in this bare awareness of thoughts, feelings, and perceptions as they occur. In the Buddhist tradition, this gentle awareness involves resting in our natural clarity. Just as in the example of crossing the bridge, if I were to become aware of each of my patterns rather than be carried away by them, their power over me would fade. I'd be able to experience their appearance as nothing more than a combination of factors, similar to the factors that cause waves to come and go across a lake, a pond, or an ocean. With the help of my teachers, I learned that that was precisely what happens in my own being whenever I approach a situation that scares or otherwise troubles me. I can become so overwhelmed by my patterns that at first I forget to *look*. But eventually I do remember what I've been taught: that simply looking at my experience begins to transform it.

GLIMPSING CLARITY

To experience clarity it is often necessary to embark on another *shinay* or *shamata* exercise, this time using a focus of attention. For the sake of simplicity, it is often recommended to focus on the breath.

Start off by sitting in a chair, on a meditation cushion, or on the floor. Take a few moments to rest in objectless *shinay* in order to open yourself to experience. Then just allow yourself to turn your attention to your breath coming in and going out. As you focus on your breathing, you'll almost inevitably find yourself distracted by all sorts of thoughts and feelings, memories and judgments—even physical sensations. Some of these may pass lightly and quickly; others may stick around for a while, attracting other thoughts, feelings, judgments, and so on. You may find yourself carried away by their sheer number and variety or by a particularly vivid train of thought.

Then all of a sudden, you'll recognize, "Oh no! I'm supposed to be focusing on my breath!"

This brief moment of recognition is, for many of us, our first taste of clarity—a flash of a "big picture" type of awareness that is capable of identifying thoughts, feelings, and sensations without identifying *with* them.

Such initial glimpses, however, are usually quite brief. When we catch ourselves being carried away by thoughts, feelings, and so on, we simply bring ourselves back to focusing on the breath. Gradually, the glimpses grow longer and the clarity that recognizes thoughts, feelings and sensations becomes more stable.

Developing such stability does take time. When I first started working with this exercise, I was quite dismayed by the sheer number and variety of thoughts, feelings, perceptions that seemed to rush through my awareness like a swollen river. I thought I was a failure. But when I asked a few of my teachers about it, they pointed out that what I was experiencing was not a failure at all but rather a sign of success: I was beginning to recognize how much stuff passed through my awareness without my even noticing it.

If I kept up this practice, I was told, I'd find that even though all sorts of thoughts and emotions might come and go, basic clarity was never disturbed or corrupted. The Buddhist texts use a number of analogies to describe this situation. One of the most vivid is the story of a traveler who arrived at the shore of a large lake on a day of calm, cool weather. The sky was cloudless and the surface of the lake was a still, clear blue. The traveler stopped that night at a nearby fisherman's hut. When he woke the next morning, the lake appeared thick and muddy.

"What happened?" he wondered. "Yesterday the lake was so clear and blue, and today it's suddenly dirty."

He walked down to the shore but couldn't see any obvious reason for the change. There wasn't any mud in the water or along the beach. Then he looked up and saw that the sky was filled with dark gray clouds. In that moment, he realized that the color of the clouds had changed the color of the lake; the water itself, when he looked closely at it, was still clean and clear.

Our essential clarity, in many ways, is like the lake. The "color" may seem to change from day to day or moment to moment, reflecting thoughts, emotions, and so on that pass "overhead," so to speak. No matter what it's reflecting, its essence never changes: It's always clean, calm, and transparent.

We often compress such experiences into a single, comprehensive whole. As one man recently said, "As a child, my life was all about being the short, fat kid—the perfect target for kids who were bigger, taller, and stronger than me. I carried that image for a lot of my adult life. But after looking at that image of myself, I began to see that it really was just an image—an idea! Hey, I'm not the fat-kid loser I thought I was. Maybe I'm something else. I don't know what, but maybe someone different."

When we become more accustomed to turning our awareness inward, however, we begin to decompress such images. The content of our awareness begins to break up into smaller pieces—the way clouds break up on a windy day, exposing here and there a glimpse of open sky. In so doing, we begin to use the process of distinction rather than being used by it. We begin to see how past experiences might turn into present patterns. We glimpse the possibility of a connection between what we see and our capacity to see.

A CHANGE IN FOCUS

I'm the type of person who likes to learn about the human mind, the human heart and how the teachings of the Buddha can transform the patterns that block our realization of well-being, which is the basis for realizing a deeper, broader awakening of our potential. In order to understand such things, I need to understand the background, the culture, the habitual patterns, the environment that shapes the lives of the people I teach. Such an understanding doesn't develop overnight, of course (at least in my case), but has to be developed over time, by watching how students respond to teachings and by listening to their questions. Through deeper understanding, I can offer teachings that meet the needs of people born and raised in different cultures.

For example, in Nepal and India, many of the people I've taught are able to connect with their emotions quite easily. They're kind, generous, and relaxed. However, I've seen that many of my students there have a hard time focusing and paying attention. They don't bother much about time and are somewhat lax in showing up for a meeting or for work. Consequently, when I teach in some Asian countries, I tend to focus on the importance of clarity and attention, on learning how to focus, to pay attention.

When I began to teach in the West, I assumed the students would share the same problems. The first few times I came to the West, I gave a lot of teachings on clarity. On the first day of teachings, I could see that the people attending had become quite focused and attentive. Then the next day, they would come back and I could see that they had sort of shut down. Yes, they were attempting to use whatever I'd taught them to become peaceful and calm, but I could tell by their posture, slack facial expressions, and closed or unfocused eyes that they were trying to suppress or ignore feelings, trying to escape them.

I thought, "Okay, something is wrong here." It took me a while to understand that the sandwich problem might be more intense in the West than in some Asian counties—that people in the West were so pressed between professional and personal demands that they didn't want to touch their feelings and consistently dimmed their awareness of them. Every year these students came back and I would give the clarity teachings, and I would find that they were soon engaged in what I call "stupid meditation."

Gradually I realized that I had to teach about the third aspect of our innate spark.

LOVE

This third aspect is traditionally translated as *compassion*—a degree of openness and intelligence that enables us to see the suffering of others and to spontaneously move to help them.

But the Tibetan term *nying-jé* indicates something much more profound. *Nying* is one of the Tibetan words for "heart." *Jé* means "noble" or "lord"—in the sense of "ruler" or "highest." Taken together, these two words suggest the highest or most noble type of heart, a profound experience and expression of connectedness, completely unencumbered by attachments or conditions.

A simpler, more direct term for this nobility of heart, so basic to our nature, is *love*.

Love is a loaded word, though, and needs to be examined closely. For example, a student of mine who'd just come out of a string of unhappy relationships recently told me, "I've had it with love. I'm just not going to be involved with anyone anymore. From now on, I'm just going to devote my life to caring for all living beings."

I looked at him for a moment and then said, "Well, that's stupid. How can you love all beings if you can't bring yourself to love just one?"

I think he was shocked; at least that was the impression I got when his jaw dropped and his eyes went wide. Perhaps he expected some sort of praise or acknowledgment for his decision to devote himself to all living beings. That is, in fact, a very noble aspiration when the motivation truly springs from that nobility of heart mentioned earlier. However, it seemed from the way this fellow expressed himself that his intention was born out of frustration or disappointment—an experience that is all too common where the heart is concerned.

Very often, the varieties of love with which we are ordinarily familiar are conditional. We tend to experience love as a kind of commodity, to be exchanged on the basis of reward and punishment: "I'll give this form of comfort in exchange for that kind." "I'll satisfy this need for you, if you satisfy that one for me." "I'll make you feel good this way, if you make me feel good that way."

Complicating things further is a somewhat more negative type of exchange, which might be politely referred to as emotional blackmail: "If you don't give me this form of comfort I crave, I won't give you the comfort you seek." "If you don't satisfy my needs, I won't satisfy yours." "If you don't make me feel good in the way I want, I won't make you feel good in the way you want."

You can supply your own script for both types of exchange, but the basic structure is, in most cases, pretty much the same. The commentary may sometimes be verbalized quite loudly (usually during emotionally charged moments), but it's not always clearly or directly articulated. Instead, our conditional love "scripts" play out as a kind of low-level background noise, similar to the security announcements broadcast in airports. The first few times we hear such announcements we might be startled or disturbed, but after hearing them a few times, we tend to tune them out.

Similarly, we tend to disregard the alarms raised about love. We don't recognize that there's something fundamentally tragic in the conditions we place upon the giving and receiving of love. We accept the love-as-commodity approach as normal—because, quite frankly, it is, in the sense that it reflects a level of understanding and behavior that is commonly, if not always consciously, adopted by millions of people around the world. But just because a way of thinking, feeling, and behaving is common doesn't necessarily mean that it's constructive.

In fact, it can become quite destructive. Gradually, when we've been disappointed many times by not being fulfilled by someone else, we lose hope that we can ever experience love in any form, and we withdraw altogether. That hopelessness, which may be called "wounded love," can set in at a very early age—especially among children brought up in abusive households and dangerous neighborhoods. It can also grow over time. Even if someone approaches us with admiration and respect, we may find ourselves incapable of accepting that warmth, we can't accept that person—because, however our wounds occur, they become part of a pattern associated with the way we think and feel about ourselves.

Such patterns emerge from social and cultural influences, as well as from personal experiences that, over time, become familiar. And questioning the familiar is almost always uncomfortable.

But that task is one that Buddha, along with so many of the world's great figures, like Mother Teresa and Martin Luther King Jr., have urged us to do. It's a task that many of the world's unsung heroes—doctors, nurses, educators, and scientists, to mention but a few—have asked us to undertake. To take another look. To let go of familiar ideas and attitudes that act in many ways like blinders on experience. To stop ignoring the announcements. To step out of our comfort zones and question what we think of as "real," or "possible," or "doable."

"You have to start somewhere," I told the man who had come to talk to me about love. "And that somewhere is *you*. If you can't love yourself, it will be very difficult for you to love anyone else."

I wasn't talking about the kind of self-love that is often confused with narcissism—a condition that, as I've learned through conversations with Western psychologists, is based on low self-esteem and a reliance on gaining a sense of recognition or power through dominating others.

I was talking about something fundamental, beyond that which, on a superficial level, can become compromised, or wounded, when we engage in the sort of give-and-take, stock market exchange of affection that is prevalent in many cultures, past and present.

ESSENCE LOVE

What I meant when speaking to this man about learning to love himself was a process that involves diving deeply into his personal experience and understanding and connecting with qualities of openness and clarity that were already a part of his nature. That openness, that clarity, offers every one of us the possibility to experience a tender, unbiased openness toward every living being, without conditions, without preconceptions.

That is my understanding of the Tibetan term *nying-jé*: an unconditional kindness, gentleness, and affection born of openness and intelligence that can be nurtured into a bright, burning flame that warms the whole world.

Nying-jé may perhaps be the closest term to describe the basic tendency of the heart to open unconditionally. I have tried, with the help of many teachers, friends, and students, to find a translation that motivates people to discover this essential aspect of their basic nature. The simplest term I've found is "essence love."

Essence love, like emptiness and clarity, stands beyond all the names we call ourselves and the roles we play in life: son, daughter, father, mother, husband, wife, and so on. It's not something manufactured, nor can it be destroyed, because it emerges spontaneously from the inseparability of emptiness and clarity, which are themselves uncreated. It may best be described as a very basic sense of well-being, which, if nurtured properly, can extend to a kinship with all other living beings. As Albert Einstein once wrote to a friend, "A human being is a part of a whole called by us the universe."

We often witness this universality when infants respond to people around them—smiling, gurgling, snuggling in someone's arms. When I held my newborn daughters, I was amazed not only by the ease with which they rested within my arms but also by the pure, reciprocal feeling of openness and affection I felt toward them—which continues to this day. I'm overjoyed to see my younger daughter laugh and play or hug a puppy in her arms; to see her bold playfulness in addressing a visitor to our home in Nepal. I'm equally amazed by my elder daughter, who in what seems to me an astonishingly short twenty years grew from an infant, to a playful girl, to a somewhat jaded teenager, and, now, to a nun.

Every Buddhist meditation practice ultimately turns toward a re-connection with essence love. When we look at our experience, very gradually we begin to recognize our similarity to those around us. When we see our own aspiration to live wholly and happily, we gradu-ally begin seeing the same longing in others. When we look clearly at our own fear, anger, or aversion, we become aware that the harsh words and actions of others are motivated by similar feelings of fear, anger, and aversion.

One of the great mistakes I've made as a teacher—and I've made many—is a failure to emphasize the importance of essence love. For many years I taught about emptiness and clarity, but until recently I didn't teach much about essence love.

But a few years ago, a British friend reminded me of the principle of making a perfect cup of tea, for which several ingredients are neces-sary: hot water, milk (or lemon, if you're a purist), sugar (sometimes), and tea.

Tea is the essential ingredient. Without it, all we have is a watery, milky (or lemony), and possibly sugary drink. In the same way, essence love may be understood as a crucial "ingredient" of our basic nature.

A TASTE OF ESSENCE LOVE

Do you want to experience a taste of essence love?

Just close your eyes for a moment and take a deep breath.

What is it you wish for?

Don't think about it, just feel it.

Chances are you feel a wish to return to a period of peace, calmness, and well-being, often couched in terms of something you experienced when you were very young. If asked, though, most of us can't remember a specific time when we experienced such feelings. Most of us don't have memories of a time when love was unconditional. Yet we all long for that unconditional well of love. And in that longing, the voice of essence love whispers that it is possible to discover it.

A connection with essence love, I've found, is best discovered through relaxation. Of course, you have to be able to bring a gentle attention to the process, like lighting a dim lamp in a quiet room. As you maintain that attention, relax . . .

Relax . . .

Relax . . .

. . . until you sense some small spark of well-being, or what might be called "okayness."

Some people find this well-being in their chest area, where the physical heart is located. Others find it in their foreheads, just a gentle loosening of tension there. One person found it in his knee, which had been troubling him for years: for a brief couple of seconds, the pain was there, but it didn't trouble him.

"Totally unexpected," he said. "Blew my mind. I thought maybe I'd have some nice, comforting memory or something. But what happened is that I had this . . . *feeling* is the best way I can describe it . . . that there was something much more to me than the pain . . . a bigger me-ness that kind of surrounded the pain, embraced it. It only lasted a few seconds—but wow!"

That is a taste of essence love: a small, bright experience of okayness. Maybe it is accompanied by some feeling of joy, but not a joy that's dependent on some thing, some person, or some condition, nothing based on external stuff—just an intrinsic feeling, however small, however dim, of well-being, some part within you that is warm and content. So connect with that.

But don't cling to it; don't try to hang on to it. Just let your awareness touch it lightly, and then let it go. If we try to hang on to it, it becomes something that we want to attach to and define and hold on to. Then it becomes frozen, a thing, some new way to identify ourselves. It's that process of relaxing until we brush against that feeling of well-being and then letting it go that actually allows the connection to become a little stronger, a little brighter, a little more a part of our everyday experience.

Every time you connect, a little bit more clarity stays around the love, a little bit more space opens up around it. Your mind becomes clearer. You experience expanded possibilities. You become a little more confident, a little more willing to connect with others, a little more willing to open up to other people, whether that means talking about your own stuff or listening to theirs. And as that happens a little miracle occurs: You're giving, without expectation of return. Your very being becomes, consciously or not, an inspiration to others.

Your spark has begun to grow.

BOUNDLESS LOVE

Although reconnecting with essence love may be part of the process of Buddhist practice of recognizing the spark within us, it's only one step in a longer and ultimately more lasting and fulfilling journey out of fear, darkness, depression, and other challenges. Everything I've learned from my teachers, my students, and my own experience agrees that the motive behind the Buddha's teachings was to cultivate a deep and active caring for the fate of all living creatures. So once we have tasted essence love—and many of the practices described in the following pages provide various means of doing so—the next step is to move beyond essence love to boundless love. One of the simplest methods for doing so is a Tibetan Buddhist practice known as *tonglen*, which can be translated as "sending and taking" and which involves a combination of breathing and visualization to send out whatever positive energy you have and whatever pain others may be feeling.

For a long time, *tonglen* was for me kind of an abstract practice: nice in principle but a little pointless. That was before my first trip to the West, at twenty-two, when I traveled to Argentina to teach.

I'd never taken a long flight anywhere and I was curious about the behavior of the Western flight attendants on the airplanes that first carried me from Delhi to London and London to Argentina. These long flights gave me an opportunity to observe how the flight attendants moved, how they served, how they acted toward passengers. Whenever an attendant approached me, I noticed that she wore a big, toothy grin as she asked me, "Sir, can I help you? Can I offer you something to eat or drink?" As soon as she turned away, I noticed that the smile disappeared. I wondered why that was—why she would smile for one second, turn away, and then stop smiling. After a few hours of this, I have to admit that I began to feel a little irritated. The smiles seemed fake, not a genuine expression of engagement but an act.

Then I landed in Argentina and was met at the airport by about forty people. All of them kissed me on both of my cheeks, which made me a little uncomfortable because I was not used to such intimate physical contact from strangers. Afterward, I asked my translator if this was the usual practice, and he said, "Yes, that's how we greet each other." I asked him to tell people that that kind of behavior made me uncomfortable. So instead of kissing me they started offering gifts.

One person, for example, brought me a feather and gave a long explanation about how the feather dropped into his lap when he heard I was coming to teach. Every gift offered was accompanied by a similar long story. In the beginning, I just accepted their gifts without listening to their stories. Sometimes people would place a gift in my hands but continue to hold on to it, not letting go, until I had listened to their story and offered a response to it. Of course, I would smile when people would approach me with these gifts. But after a while, I felt my mouth and my cheeks begin to freeze into a position that wasn't necessarily genuine but seemed to be expected and desired by the people offering gifts.

During this time, a person who accompanied me was taking pictures of these gift-giving occasions. When I got back to Nepal, I looked through the photograph album and saw the same sort of bright, toothy grin on my own face that I'd seen on the airline attendants, and my irritation melted away. I thought, "Oh, they're busy. They're walking around, dealing with turbulence, unhappy passengers, but they're still trying to smile, to be pleasant even in difficult circumstances."

That was a big lesson for me. I can't know, I can't judge, I can't teach until I know and understand other people's experience. So I try my best to understand not only big cultural differences but also the individual experiences of the people I meet.

After that, *tonglen* assumed a more personal dimension for me as a practice. Before you can really begin to understand the challenges another person faces you need to understand them yourself—not just intellectually but in your gut. By that time I'd experienced a few things—anxiety, illness, depression, ridicule, humiliation—but it was the airline attendants' gracious attempts to appear pleasant in very difficult circumstances that gave me a sense of the practicality of *tonglen*.

Often overlooked in the instructions of *tonglen* is that the most fruitful time to practice it is when we're feeling bad about ourselves—

when we're consumed by anger, despair, jealousy, or some other negative feeling. We take these feelings, and our desire to get past them, as a starting point.

Begin by finding a restful position for your body and allow yourself to rest a few moments in objectless *shinay*.

Breathe in; breathe out.

Let yourself feel the weight of whatever you're experiencing.

Let yourself recognize that you're being unkind to yourself, that somehow you've blocked your innate sense of well-being.

Breathe in and out again, but this time engage your imagination.

Bring your attention to the person or persons who have brought about a painful situation—it might be a lover, a spouse, a coworker, or a child.

Breathe in all the darkness and pain that may have caused that person to act that way. Imagine it as a dark greasy cloud of oily smoke.

Breathe out brightness—the essence of your own spark—and imagine it filling that person with confidence, light, a connection to essence love.

Keep doing this until you feel quite sure that the person toward whom you have some difficult thoughts and feelings will somehow, through his or her own path, reconnect with his or her own spark.

This practice may be difficult at first. Many people I've spoken with over the past years were emotionally, physically, or sexually abused by people they trusted, people who misused or betrayed positions of trust. And the horrors they inflicted upon the people who trusted them can't be denied.

Tonglen is not a practice of forgiving or forgetting. Rather, it is a practice that provides us with the capability of rising beyond the personal pain that we have endured and restoring confidence in our ability to face challenges; that we can move beyond it and learn to live productive, fulfilling lives.

The next step in the *tonglen* process is to bring your attention to this thought: "Just as I want to reconnect with my spark, other beings also feel the same way." You don't need to visualize specific beings, although you may start out with a specific visualization if you find it helpful.

Tonglen extends beyond those you don't know personally, individuals who have experienced pain or will experience pain in any way. The point, as I was taught, is simply to remember that the world is filled with an infinite number of beings and to think that all of them in their own way are living creatures who just want to live and thrive. Just as you wish to live without pain, all living creatures seek the same goal. Just as you wish to avoid pain, disappointment, jealousy, illness, and death, all beings wish to avoid the same sort of disillusionment that comes from losing our connection to essence love. As you allow these thoughts to roll around in your heart you'll actually begin to find yourself actively engaged in wishing for others' happiness and freedom from pain.

The next step is to focus on your breathing as a means of sending whatever happiness you may have experienced or are currently experiencing to all living beings and absorb their suffering. As you exhale, imagine all the happiness and benefits you've acquired during your life pouring out of yourself in the form of clear light. This light extends out toward all beings and dissolves into them, fulfilling all their needs and eliminating their pain. As you inhale, imagine the pain and suffering of all living beings as a dark, oily smoke being absorbed through your nostrils and dissolving into your heart. As you exhale, imagine a bright light surrounding and filling them. Imagine that all these countless beings are freed from their patterns and able to connect with essence love.

After practicing in this way for a few moments, simply allow your mind to rest in objectless *shinay*, just allowing yourself to watch whatever you're experiencing. Maybe you'll find a little sense of realization and relief, a little opening of the heart, a recognition that whatever your condition, whatever challenges you face, you're not alone.

BODHICITTA

Boundless love is yet another step in the direction of actualizing our full potential. The final step involves becoming fully awake, fully able to do whatever we can do to bring a halt to the terrible bickering that leads to wars, both global and personal, and usher in an era of peace and contentment that most of us consider a distant fantasy.

This unconditional wakefulness is described in the Sanskrit term *bodhicitta*, a word made up of two words. The first is *bodhi*, which, as mentioned earlier, is a Sanskrit and a Pali word derived from the root term *budh*. *Bodhi* is often translated as "awake" or "awakened"—a profound and vibrant alertness that absolutely cuts through all the mental and emotional residue that tends to cloud our normal awareness. It's a state of awareness in which we see quite clearly the various strategies we typically adopt in order to get through the day.

We all experience little awakenings of this sort—we could call them "buddha moments." For example, when we're stuck in traffic and find ourselves cursing other drivers, we might experience a lightning recognition of how lucky we are to have a car, to be going somewhere to meet someone. When we grumble about children who need attention—for whatever reason, homework, meals, school tuition—we wake up suddenly to the realization of how fortunate we are that these bright, young, capable people are a part of our lives.

Buddha moments may sometimes be uncomfortable on the surface but are ultimately quite liberating. They offer us an opportunity to get to know the angry thoughts and feelings that drive our behavior, and to welcome them as friends that point out areas of limiting thoughts and feelings rather than dismissing them as enemies. If we pay attention to these buddha moments, very gradually we can begin to grow toward a bigger, brighter, broader way of living.

THE HEART OF THE MATTER

The second part of this deep and active caring is *citta* (pronounced "chitta"), a word often translated on a literal level as "mind." On a more subtle level, however, the word *citta* can also be understood as "heart"— not the physical organ that pumps blood through our bodies but rather the aspect of our nature that directs our thoughts, moods, and behavior.

Let me explain.

In some languages, "mind" and "heart" are closely related terms, often used interchangeably. For example, people may refer to someone who acts with good intentions as a person who has his or her "heart in the right place."

In the Tibetan language, moreover, the similarity between "mind" and "heart" becomes apparent through the confusion it offers to people from other cultures. Several years ago, for example, a student of mine accompanied a doctor on a trip to Tibet. Many of the patients who came to the free medical clinics described a problem they were suffering from as "low *sem*"—*sem* being the word most frequently used to describe the whole system of thinking and perceiving. They pointed to their heart area as the source of their difficulties. The doctor, after measuring their blood pressure and using a stethoscope to measure their heart rates, found no irregularities. Only after lengthy discussions with translators did she begin to understand that the problem described to her was not related to the actual organ of the heart. The "low *sem*" people were describing was actually a form of depression—what might be described as a "heavy heart."

In Tibetan Buddhist rituals, moreover, one points to the heart when reciting the word *mind*. Even in casual conversation many Tibetan people point to their hearts when referring to their minds.

That the words *mind* and *heart* may be used interchangeably in many languages suggests to me a broad cultural agreement that they are both understood as the central location of all our ideas, judgments, opinions, and so on. So whether we're talking about *bodhicitta* as "awakened mind" or "awakened heart," we're really taking about the same experience of something essential waking up and crying out for attention.

When my daughters woke up crying in the middle of the night, either my wife or I would rush into their room, pick them up, cradle them, and—depending on the situation—change their diapers or feed them (or both). It was an instant response of the heart or the mind to soothe and comfort a being in distress.

Sometimes cradling my daughters, feeding them, or changing their diapers wasn't enough to stop their crying, but we did our best—verbally (repeating the soothing mantras known to every parent, in every language) and nonverbally (holding them, patting them, rocking them—physical actions that would alleviate their distress).

To me this is the real meaning of *bodhicitta*: waking to a cry in the darkness and responding to the best of our abilities.

The only difference is that, in the case of *bodhicitta, we* ourselves are often the ones crying in the dark. Unfortunately, we tend to sleep through the conflicts we face in our lives. We ignore our buddha moments and don't let them awaken our hearts. We fail to see that recognizing, admitting, and clearly understanding the patterns we experience in our own lives can have a transformative effect on the way we function in the world and the way we relate to others.

ABSOLUTE AND RELATIVE

According to the Buddha and the great masters who followed in his footsteps, there are two types, or levels, of *bodhicitta*: absolute and relative. Absolute *bodhicitta* is a spontaneous recognition that all sentient beings, regardless of how we act or appear, are already completely free from whatever limits the patterns in our lives seemingly impose on us. It is a deep and penetrating vision into the nature of existence; a recognition that, despite what we believe about ourselves, we are, in essence, already enlightened. In fact it is the openness and freedom of our enlightened nature that, in a peculiar way, allows us to manifest the patterns that seem so debilitating.

A person who has attained absolute *bodhicitta* sees everyone, deep in their natures, as fully awakened beings and quite naturally treats them with deep respect. Within absolute *bodhicitta*, or the absolutely awakened heart, there is no distinction between subject and object, self and other. All sentient beings are spontaneously recognized as perfect manifestations of basic nature.

When we encounter people who have attained this level of awakened heart we sense a degree of kindness, generosity, and patience that stirs something deep with ourselves. We feel lighter, brighter, a bit more open to others and more forgiving to what we have typically considered faults or flaws within ourselves and others.

Developing absolute *bodhicitta* within our own experience evolves through nurturing another, more accessible aspect known as relative *bodhicitta*. Most simply understood, relative *bodhicitta* involves sincerely dedicating ourselves toward helping all sentient beings to become completely free of suffering through recognizing their true nature. This effort is referred to as relative, because it is still grounded in a dualistic perception of reality in which subjects and objects, selves and others—as well as various characteristics of experience, such as good and bad, pleasant and unpleasant—are defined and experienced in relation to one another.

To use an analogy, absolute *bodhicitta* is like the top of a tree, while relative *bodhicitta* may be compared to the roots, trunk, and lower branches. All of them are parts of the same tree, but each stands in a relative relationship to the topmost branches. If we want to reach the top branches, we have to climb through all of the lower parts.

ASPIRATION AND APPLICATION

I should mention here that relative *bodhicitta* is divided further into two aspects: aspiration *bodhicitta* and application *bodhicitta*. We begin by thinking, at the beginning of each session of meditation practice, that we aspire to awaken in order to help all beings attain the same state of openness. In the Buddhist tradition, it's common to begin by reciting a small prayer to the effect that whatever efforts we exert will be of some benefit to others.

At the end of our practice, it's traditional to pass whatever strength, peace, or calmness we've awakened on to others.

Of course, some people may balk at this. "Why should I give away the work I've done to people I don't know?"

All I can tell you is that you don't lose anything by sharing. Strength grows by giving it away.

You can see it for yourself the next time you enter a fast-food restaurant and look into the eyes of someone taking your order for a meal. Maybe they'll seem a bit more alive and alert when fulfilling your order. Or maybe when you genuinely thank someone who fills your gas tank, you can see his eyes light up, his body straighten as he genuinely recognizes that someone is seeing him as a human being. Perhaps he will be more likely to address the next person he serves as a human being—acting more kindly and politely—which may influence the behavior of the person served to treat the next person he or she meets with an extra degree of courtesy and respect. I've seen people, too, who thank a bus driver when getting off a bus. Sometimes there's no reaction, but as other people take note of that action and thank the bus driver too, an atmosphere of good feeling ripples through the bus and, perhaps, spreads out across the city.

In this sense, aspiration *bodhicitta* is like focusing on the goal of carrying everyone to a certain destination—for example, London, Paris, or Washington, D.C. In the case of aspiration *bodhicitta*, of course, the "destination" is the total awakening of the mind, or absolute *bodhicitta*. Application *bodhicitta* involves actually taking the steps to arrive at an intended destination. It focuses on the path of attaining the goal of aspiration *bodhicitta*: freeing all living beings from suffering through recognition of their basic nature.

REMEMBERING

Many of us may wonder, if we're capable of so much, why aren't we all living joyfully, openly, and peacefully together? Why is there so much war, violence, and tragedy in the world? Why do some of us feel hollow inside? Why do we feel jealous, angry, afraid, depressed, even suicidal? Why do we argue with the people we're closest to? Why do we race around so much, jumping from relationship to relationship, job to job, always looking for the next best thing, the newest gadget? Why do some of us turn to alcohol, or drugs, or sex, or food? Why do we punish ourselves, our children, our friends? Why do we feel so limited and powerless?

The simplest answer is that we've forgotten who we are. That basis of openness, clarity, and love gets layered over—in part by the way we are structured as human beings and in part by our experiences and the lessons we learn throughout life.

There's an old Buddhist story about a wrestler who wore a jewel in his hair. During a match with other wrestlers, he received a blow to his head, and without his realizing it, the jewel dropped into the wound. When the wound healed over, the jewel was covered up by the scar. The poor wrestler spent the rest of his days looking for the jewel, never realizing that it was inside him all the time.

That's the position in which most of us find ourselves. We believe deep down that we've lost something precious and are seeking it outside ourselves, never realizing that we are carrying it within us wherever we go.

But if we just look beneath the scars, the wounds we've experienced in life, we can rediscover that jewel, that basic, unconditional love. We can clean and polish it until all its facets sparkle. In the same way, when we rediscover essence love, we can nurture and cultivate it until it becomes *bodhicitta*, a deep and active caring for the welfare others.

Of course, developing *bodhicitta* often requires some sacrifice, a decision to place the well-being of another above our own desires, needs, hopes, and fears. It means granting people the right to make their own decisions even if we don't agree with them. It means allowing people to make mistakes and allowing them to learn from them. It means accepting what we may consider "flaws" in our own and others' personalities and accepting them as part of a larger, long-term learning process. It means cultivating within ourselves a place of deep caring, a sense of "home" to which we can always return, be welcome, and rediscover the capacity for healing from whatever hurt we've caused ourselves and others. Through this healing, we begin to approach a greater potential as human beings than we could ever have imagined.

Questions remain, though: How do we awaken? How do we light up?

The answers can be found in the following chapters, which provide some basic insights into the Buddhist understanding of how human development in general and events in our own lives come together to layer over our spark. They also provide practices that can begin to gently, kindly address these layers and help us to integrate what we've learned from them rather that reject them outright. There is so much we've learned from the lives we've led, and it would be a shame to simply throw it all away because of the losses we've suffered, the pain we've experienced. We've each in our own way learned a few things that might help other people.

That is one of the fundamental goals of the Buddhist path: to help people live more openly, wisely, and generously toward themselves and others. Both understanding and practice are necessary to reconnect with the spark at the basis of being and encourage it to grow. There's an old Buddhist saying that in order to fly, a bird needs two wings. In order to break through the layers of misidentification that bind us to ideas about ourselves as vulnerable, weak, unworthy, ugly, and so on, we need both an understanding of our basic nature and the patterns that keep us from expressing it, and the means of working with those patterns as kindly and gently as possible.

In the meantime, I'd like to give you another taste of what this experience of clarity and warmth may be like.

FEATHERS

I've been fortunate in having met and been taught by people who have genuinely cultivated *bodhicitta*. One of the clearest examples was my father, Tulku Urgyen Rinpoche, a great teacher who possessed a sort of wisdom rarely seen in modern times. People from all over the world came to visit him at his hermitage of Nagi Gompa, a nunnery and retreat center high on the northern slopes of the Kathmandu valley. Built in the mid-1960s, Nagi Gompa was one of the first centers of learning and practice to emerge in Nepal after the political changes across Tibet compelled many revered teachers to leave their homeland in order to preserve, protect, and pass on the learning and traditions of Tibetan Buddhism.

My father was already known in Tibet as one of the greatest teachers of the twentieth century. Born in Kham in eastern Tibet, he was recognized by the Fifteenth Karmapa as the reincarnation of both Chöwang Tulku—one of the foremost *tertöns* of the thirteenth century C.E.—and of Nubchen Sangye Yeshe, one of Guru Rinpoche's principal students. He was trained in both the Kagyu and Nyingma teachings and became well-known for his ability to transmit, in a very simple, lucid, and gently humorous style, the essence of the Buddha's original teachings and the commentaries written by later masters. His encyclopedic knowledge was impressive: He could quote just about any text as an example to illustrate an important point. But what I found most remarkable in his teaching style—aside from his great patience and genuine enjoyment in passing along the teachings—was his ability to synthesize so many different points and effortlessly present them in a way that suited the disposition of any student who heard him.

When it was learned that he had survived the political turmoil in Tibet and had safely established himself in Nepal, he was one of the "must-see" teachers for anyone traveling through Nepal. His reputation lay not only in his personal brilliance and the depth of his understanding but also in his extraordinarily open heart and his willingness to pass on everything he knew to the most untutored beginner. He did this without any sense of urgency but with a sense that whatever he passed on would help those who came to him for understanding and help disseminate the precious teachings of Tibetan Buddhism.

Great masters of the Buddhist tradition, spiritual pilgrims, and Western students of Buddhism came to study with him at Nagi Gompa because his mind was so broad and his understanding so deep. He even attracted students of neuroscience and psychology, such as Francisco Varela and Daniel Goleman, not because he was a scientist in the Western tradition but because his insights into the nature of the mind and his generosity in sharing them provided lines of inquiry that would later bear fruit in the development of contemporary research on the impact of Buddhist meditation on changing the function and structure of the brain and on developing treatment methods in standard psychological practice.

My father never turned away a student or visitor, especially those who had traveled a long distance to see him. Near the end of his life, he grew thinner and weaker; he was nevertheless kind and full of laughter. Though his doctors urged him to rest and conserve his strength, he continued to receive visitors. He posted a nun on his balcony to look out for the approach of his doctors, his attendants, and his own children. When one of us approached, she would run in to warn him and the visitor would be quickly and quietly spirited away.

More often than not, we were fooled by his game. When we entered his room, we saw a kind, old, dying man resting comfortably in his bed, his gentle smile hiding a colossal laughter born in the fires of boundless love. I think we all knew that he would never stop teaching, never stop giving. He'd taken to heart the Buddha's first teaching: that while for most of us life is full of discomfort, pain, and sorrow, there's a very practical means of transcending these experiences. The means is not always easy—it requires effort. But my father believed with his whole heart that deep within us lies a spark of openness, love, and clarity that can't be dimmed and that can be kindled to warm not only our own lives and the lives of people to whom we feel close but the entire world.

Long ago, he taught me an exercise that helped me to feel this spark, which I offer to you. You can try it anywhere, but it's probably best at the beginning to try it out in a quiet place, without too much distraction. You can do it sitting, standing, or lying down; it doesn't matter. The goal is not to become a perfect meditator but just to connect with your basic love, openness, and clarity.

Normally our awareness is overwhelmed by hundreds of different thoughts, feelings, and sensations. Some we latch on to because they're attractive fantasies or scary preoccupations; some we try to shove away because they're too upsetting or because they distract us from whatever we're trying to accomplish at the moment.

Instead of focusing on some of them and pushing away others, though, just look at them as feathers flying in the wind. The wind is your awareness, your inborn openness and clarity. Feathers—the thoughts, emotions, and physical sensations that pass through our awareness— are harmless. Some may be more attractive than others, some less attractive; but essentially they're just feathers. Look at them as fuzzy, curly things floating through the air.

As you do so, you begin to identify with the awareness that is watching the feathers and allow yourself to be okay with whatever feathers happen to be flying at the time. You're accepting them without latching on to them or trying to shove them away. This simple act of acceptance— which may only last a few seconds—offers a taste of that open space of essence love, an acceptance of the warmth that is your basic nature, the heart of your own being.

This heart, this openness, this clarity is completely "I"-less: a center-less center that is rather difficult to explain in words in the sense that it's not identified with any specific being, raised in a particular culture, in a particular neighborhood, with any set of conditions.

When we're born into bodies, into cultures, into familial relationships, however, we become conditioned, and as a consequence, we begin to experience limitations. We lose our sense of openness and freedom. Our spark does not go out, but it seems to grow a little dim.

Fortunately, we can begin to lift those limitations. We can reconnect with our innate openness and clarity, and experience the full warmth and brilliance of our spark. In order to do so, we need to understand how we managed to lose touch with those essential aspects of ourselves to begin with.

FOUR

Mis"I"dentification

Many of us share a tendency to see certain things as more solid and real than may actually be the case. Particularly in these difficult times, I've heard many people say that they're terrified of calling their credit card companies or tax collection agencies to discuss outstanding balances. But when they do summon the courage to contact these companies and agencies, many times they find someone who is deeply sympathetic, someone who says, "I understand what you're going through, and I want to help."

The social and economic challenges from which many people are suffering in recent days are quite similar to the challenges that many people in times past have faced. Ultimately such challenges have produced people who have broken through rigid walls of understanding and belief in order to enhance and expand their relationships with *people*: not as individuals bound by circumstances but as living, moving, imaginative beings. By even considering the possibility of opening your heart and mind you have become one of these extraordinary individuals who make a positive difference, not only in their own lives but in the lives of others.

Walls have existed in many different societies across millennia. But every once in a while walls that seem quite strong—sometimes on a personal level and sometimes on a communal, cultural level—can crumble.

Let me give you a small, personal example.

THE TRAIN

For four years after my father received the letter from the Karmapa identifying me as a *tulku,* my childhood continued pretty much as it had. I spent the summers in Nubri, where the weather was cool relative to much of Nepal. During the winter months, my mother, my grandfather, my younger brother, and I would travel to my father's hermitage, Nagi Gompa, a bit south of Nubri, where the winter weather was somewhat less intense.

Then one day, when I was twelve years old, my father received another letter, this time from the eighth Khamtrul Rinpoche, the head of Tashi Jong monastery in northern India. His letter indicated in rather strong terms that I should be sent to Tashi Jong monastery for training. It was not so much an invitation as an order.

To put this order in context, I should explain that, according to Tibetan Buddhist tradition, a great master transmits everything he's learned—including very personal, private insights—to one or two senior students, who will then act as the principal tutor to the next incarnation of his own teacher.

I know this type of learning may seem strange to many people, but it makes some sense in terms of a larger context of parents transmitting, verbally or nonverbally, their experiences and values to their children. Something vital is transferred in this kind of verbal and nonverbal communication, a connection that is intellectual and emotional, yet at the same time transcends both categories.

In my own case, the sixth Khamtrul Rinpoche, Tenpa Nyima, had been the principal student of the first Tsoknyi Rinpoche and had received all of his teachings and instructions. The second Tsoknyi Rinpoche had been a student of Tenpa Nyima, and had received from him the major teachings passed down and preserved by the first Tsoknyi Rinpoche. So there was a deep connection between the lineages of Khamtrul Rinpoches and Tsoknyi Rinpoches. Accordingly, the eighth Khamtrul Rinpoche felt a strong duty to direct my training.

After a few weeks of preparation, my grandfather and I, along with several elders from the village in which I was raised, set out on the long journey to India. It took eight days to go from Nubri to Kathmandu by foot, then a day or so to travel by bus from Kathmandu to the Indian border. From there, we took a train down into India.

I had never seen a train before. I'd heard about trains from my grandfather, who'd traveled on one several years earlier. He described it as something like a line of houses, each about the size of ours in Nubri, which traveled on wheels along metal rails.

The image worried me. How could a house move on wheels without cracking and breaking? I approached the possibility of traveling in a house on wheels with some trepidation, influenced by imagination.

When I saw the train with my own eyes, I realized it was made of metal, not wood and stone, and my notion of traveling in a moving house was put to rest by actual experience.

It was then that I began to discern the difference between imagination and reality—the beginning of a long process that has led me to understand that the ideas about who we are and what we're capable of achieving are based on misconceptions, on stories we're told by others, enhanced by the fertility of imagination that is one of the gifts of openness and clarity.

"I"MAGINATION

After the train ride, we took another bus that would carry us closer to
Tashi Jong. The bus let us off about twenty minutes from the monastery, but even at that distance I could hear, faintly, the sound of a conch
shell being blown like trumpet—signaling the beginning of a group
practice. As we drew closer, walking across a grassy plain lightly moist-
ened by rain, I could hear the monks chanting. After days of traveling,
hearing these sounds, familiar to me from the years I'd spent in and
around monastic communities, my fears began to subside somewhat.
Though far from the little house I shared with my family in Nepal, I
felt like I was coming home.

Tashi Jong—which in Tibetan means "auspicious valley"—is a
sprawling monastery complex, surrounded by a large community of
Tibetans in exile. It's rather famous for its *tokdens*, meditation masters
who spend long years in solitary retreat perfecting their practice so that
the teachings of the Buddha become more than just nice words and
interesting concepts but are a living part of their being. During periods
when they emerge from retreat, many of them serve as teachers; some
perform other duties necessary to running a large monastery. During
my time there, I began to see that they also served as extraordinary
examples of the realization of human potential. Wise, kind, and patient, they had not only nurtured their inner spark but had fanned it
into a burning flame that served as an inspiration to the students at the
monastery and to the surrounding community.

Tashi Jong was famous for another reason, as well. It had been
founded by the eighth Khamtrul Rinpoche—the same man who had
sent the letter to my father commanding me to come there for training.
One of the great meditation masters of the twentieth century, Kham-

trul Rinpoche was also a brilliant scholar and artist who had overseen one of the largest monasteries in eastern Tibet, as well as more than two hundred small monasteries. He had remained in eastern Tibet through much of the turmoil that erupted during the 1950s, but after realizing that the various resistance movements that had arisen there would be crushed, he made the difficult decision to leave for India with sixteen monks and *tulkus* in order to preserve the precious lineage of learning that had been passed down to him.

Khamtrul Rinpoche was not in residence when we arrived, so for ten days we stayed with a family in the nearby community of Bir. I was terrified of meeting him. He was a legendary figure. When he returned and I met him for the first time, I admit that I was a bit overwhelmed. He was about forty-five years old at the time. A tall man with close-cropped dark hair, he had a commanding presence and the type of charisma that one associates with royalty. At the same time, his personal strength was tempered by a compassion that radiated through his eyes, his expressions, the gentle way he moved, sat, and gestured, and the light, mellow sound of his voice. With exquisite courtesy, he addressed my grandfather, asking about the journey. From time to time he looked at me and smiled, and even laughed, as if he knew that the first encounter between a twelve-year-old boy and one of the most powerful figures in Tibetan Buddhism might be a little uncomfortable.

And it was uncomfortable, but not for the reasons you might think.

I didn't want to be a monk. I didn't want to be *tulku*. I wanted more than anything to go back to Nepal and play with my village friends.

But every once in a while I caught a glimmer in his eye, a humorous twist in his smile, that seemed to say, "Get ready to learn how to really play. The little games you've been involved in are nothing compared to what you're going to take part in, in the village we call the world."

A day or so after Khamtrul Rinpoche's return to Tashi Jong, I was formally enthroned: a kind of inauguration ceremony, in which a *tulku* is seated on a throne, which is a symbol of his authority to teach. On the journey to India, I'd worried about what the ceremony would involve. But it turned out to be very simple: I was dressed in especially grand monastic robes, and my head was shaved, except for a small patch that was to be cut during the ceremony as a token of my commitment. Then I took my seat on the throne and Khamtrul Rinpoche offered prayers and blessings, and formally announced that I was the reincarnation of the second Tsoknyi Rinpoche. Afterward, the residents of the monastery and the people in the surrounding villages offered ceremonial gifts, and that was it. It was not the kind of enthronement ceremony that a lot of *tulkus* have to undergo. It was very simple, in keeping with Khamtrul Rinpoche's easygoing, direct style.

After the ceremony ended, he told me how happy he was that I'd finally arrived. "I know your father," he said, "and I'm so happy to continue the relationship with him through you." Then he hugged me and lifted me up into the air. His kindness, playfulness, and joy were very comforting. In just those first days of being with him, I felt as though I was in the presence of family.

Immediately after the enthronement I was placed in a small house with a monk, three other *tulkus*, and a highly revered *tokden* named Tselwang Rindzin, who served as my principal tutor during the years I spent at Tashi Jong. A rather tiny man, with short white hair and a wispy beard and mustache, Tselwang Rindzin almost never smiled. He constantly drilled us in spelling, grammar, vocabulary, and the memorization of thousands of pages of texts. But he showed his kindness in many ways—washing our clothes, making our beds, taking care of all of our needs like a concerned mother. During the night he'd prowl around the bedroom to make sure our blankets covered us completely.

At twelve years old, I didn't embrace any of the upcoming events with joy or anticipation; rather, I felt a fear bordering on terror. What I'd imagined took over my mind and my heart. When I was confronted by the reality of certain situations, however—that a train was not a stone house, for example; that Khamtrul Rinpoche swung me in his arms and told me how happy he was to see me; that Tselwang Rindzin, despite his perpetual frown, was one of the most caring people I've ever had the privilege to know—I was confused.

Questions consumed me for much of the time I spent at Tashi Jong. Slowly, however, through the patience of my teachers and the understandings and practices I learned during my time there, I began to distinguish between reality and imagination—or to put it in classic Buddhist terms, between reality and what *appears* to us as reality, which includes, among other things, our images of ourselves.

"I" STORIES

Many of us believe that we're "stone houses," likely to fall apart as soon as we begin moving. We fear that when we face unfamiliar situations we're going to encounter opposition, maybe even cruelty. As we go through life, we accumulate layers of ideas about who we are and what we're capable of achieving. In most cases these layers accumulate unconsciously: partly as a result of the way our brains and bodies are structured, partly as a result of cultural conditioning, and partly as result of the structure of language itself, which is built on making distinctions.

As these layers accumulate, we tend to become increasingly rigid in our identification with certain views about ourselves and the world around us. Gradually, we lose our connection to the basic openness, clarity, and love that is the essence of our being. We learn to define ourselves, and we hold on to such definitions even if they're unflattering or self-destructive. This "I" maintenance program can influence our thoughts, feelings, and behavior for many years.

For example, a student recently confessed, "I grew up in the 1950s being constantly teased, bullied, and made to feel as if something was terribly wrong with me. Wherever I went, people whispered about me or sometimes even physically attacked me. I didn't understand why this was happening until I was about fifteen and realized: 'Oh, God, no, I'm attracted to *boys*. And everyone can see it.'

"I hated myself. Everything I'd learned up to that point said that this attraction was not natural. That I was going to suffer for it and burn in hell.

"So I took the simple route. I denied it. I pretended the attraction wasn't there. Instead I developed a 'macho,' straight personality. I got married, fathered two children, and then got divorced.

"I'm lucky in many ways because my wife was very understanding and so are my kids. But I can't let go of the feeling that something is wrong with me. I can't let go of the shame of lying to a wonderful woman, two bright kids, and a host of friends and family members for so many years. I can't let go of the shame of creating a 'false persona' and trying to live with it for decades.

"I'm still afraid that when I come across a couple of people whispering in the office where I work that they're whispering about me.

"That's probably very egocentric, of course," he continued. "There are plenty of things my colleagues could be whispering about. I doubt that I'm very high on the 'gossip list.' But I can't seem to shake the shame or the fear or the sense of low self-esteem that I'm not 'normal.'"

When I hear the stories that some people tell about their lives, I feel like crying about the amount of shame, fear, and sadness people experience. But these people don't come to me for tears. They want advice. They want to know how to move forward in their lives, to connect with the warmth, openness, and possibility that they know, on an intuitive level, is possible. They want—as most of us do—a remedy for the pain they experience. But applying the remedy involves some understanding of how and why we arrived in such difficult situations in the first place.

BALANCING TWO REALITIES

Many of the conflicts and challenges we experience arise because, whether we know it or not, we're constantly juggling two different realities. The first is known in the Buddhist tradition as "absolute reality," which may be understood as emptiness—the indefinable, infinitely open, limitless potential for anything to appear, disappear, change, and reappear. It's because the ground, or absolute, nature of reality is unlimited that phenomena—a general term that includes thoughts, emotions, sensations, and even material objects—can appear, move, change, and ultimately vanish.

One way to understand absolute reality is through using the analogy of space as it was understood in the Buddha's time—a vast openness that is not a thing in itself but rather an infinite, uncharacterized background against and through which the sun, the moon, the stars, as well as animals, human beings, rivers, trees, and so forth appear and move. Without space, there would be no room for anything to appear, no background against which things could be seen.

At the same time, it would be absurd to deny that we live in a world in which things appear, change, and disappear in space and time. People come and go; relationships shift and change; thoughts and emotions move endlessly through our awareness; someone drinks a glass of water, and the water is absorbed into the body, nourishes cells, and is eventually voided. In Buddhist terms, this level of endlessly changing experience is known as "relative reality," or sometimes as "conventional reality." It is a level of experience that is fundamentally characterized by dualistic perception: subject and object, friend and enemy, self and other, good and bad. On this level of reality, phenomena are understood as relative because they are defined by their relation to other phenomena. A "positive" thought is distinguished by its difference from a "negative" thought, just as a short person may be defined as "short" only in relation to someone who is taller. Alone, that person is neither tall nor short. Similarly, a thought or a feeling can't, in itself, be described as positive or negative except through comparison with another thought. As I was taught, this level of reality is referred to as conventional because it is the way most beings experience reality.

The relationship between absolute and relative reality might be a little hard to understand in abstract, philosophical terms. I find it easier to explain in terms of the simple analogy of watching a movie or a television show, where we get caught up in the story. We feel an emotional and perhaps intellectual and sensual involvement. At the same time, in the back of our minds, we *know* it's a movie or a TV show, so there's a little bit of distance, a little bit of awareness that the movie is not your life. However, if that sentiment, "Oh, it's only a movie," were to dominate, we wouldn't be able to enjoy it as much, we wouldn't be caught up in it.

A similar situation occurs for most of us in our daily lives—with one significant exception. As we go about our daily lives, that little "back of the mind" awareness gets clouded over. We become completely caught up in the movie of relative reality.

How does this happen, though, and why?

"MERE I"

When we come into being on the physical level, we're clothed in a body that includes not just our physical form but a capacity to sense, to feel, and to discern. During the first months of life, however, all these aspects of embodied being are rather hazy and indistinct. Our spark becomes a bit dimmed as we become identified with our senses and our first, groping attempts to identify with the sensations passing through our awareness.

In Tibetan Buddhist terms, this state of affairs is referred to as *lhen-kyé-ma-rig-pa*—a fundamental ignorance that emerges simultaneously with sentience and leads to confusion and uncertainty about the way things are. We know, for instance, that *something* is occurring, but we can't necessarily define what it is. The classic Buddhist example is seeing a sort of coiled multicolored thing in the distance or in the dark. We can't tell whether it's a multicolored rope or a snake until conditions becomes clearer.

This situation is a good description of the first layer of "self," referred to in Tibetan as *dak tsam,* or "mere I." *Dak* is a traditional Tibetan word for "self" or "I." *Tsam* has a variety of meanings, like "approximately" or "about that much."

When connected with *dak,* however, *tsam* takes on a somewhat a more specific meaning as "mere" or "just about." When we look at the term *dak tsam,* then, we're looking at an experience that is almost "I," a fluid sense of being that might best be described as a stream of experiences, such as warmth and coldness, comfort and discomfort, sleepiness and alertness.

At this stage in our development, we have no words or labels for the things we experience or for the self that is experiencing. Nevertheless, at the level of the "mere I," we're able to discern some sense of difference: for instance, the distinction between being hungry or full, the sound of Mommy's voice and Daddy's voice, whether we're lying still or being carried or moved around, or whether we're alone or not.

But the distinctions made at the level of the "mere I" are very light. They run into a sort of continuous and continuously changing movie in which we're fully and vividly immersed. And at this point it's completely *our* movie. People, objects, sounds, smells, and so on have no independent existence of their own, nor are our experiences independent from us.

The very lightness of the "mere I" leaves a lot of space for essence love and openness to flow. There were times, for instance, when I was holding my daughters as infants that I actually felt comforted by them. I marveled at how easily they smiled, how peacefully they slept. As they grew a little bit older, they were always reaching, touching, and watching, absorbing and exploring everything they encountered with uninhibited curiosity—which can be understood as an active aspect of the native intelligence referred to earlier as clarity.

But even as a doting father, I could see that this embodiment, this immersion in sensory experience, could possibly lead to trouble. I tried my best to let my daughters just develop freely. My elder daughter left her bedroom a mess, with clothing and other stuff scattered all over the place. I figured that once she found a boyfriend she would start to clean up her room. She was kind of a free-spirited child, much as I was. Little did I suspect that she would become a nun, with few possessions and a huge sense of discipline. I sometimes worry about my younger daughter because she's a little bit wild. But she is so open and friendly. I have no idea what she will become: perhaps a scientist or a teacher. Right now she adores puppies, enjoys talking to visitors at our home in Nepal, and likes playing games. I strive my best to allow her the freedom she needs to grow into the adult she will eventually become.

But change is unpredictable and appearances are indeterminate, and we have to respect all possibilities. In order to understand how the next layer of "I" develops, we need to examine change—and our response to it—a little more closely.

CHANGE

Over the years, I've come to develop a deep respect for emptiness and for the conditions that effect changes in the realm of relative reality. Everything we experience on a day-to-day basis is subject to change. Some of the changes are obvious: Food prices change. College tuitions change. Gas prices change. The life choices of your children change. Clothes and sheets get rumpled or stained. Paint chips off furniture. Someone bumps into your car and causes a dent or a scratch.

Some changes, of course, are less immediately noticeable: The cells of our bodies, for instance, change moment by moment. Modern physics has demonstrated that molecules, atoms, and subatomic particles are constantly rearranging themselves and that objects that appear solid, like a desk, a pen, or a piece of paper, are in a constant state of flux.

Our emotional outlook shifts, too, depending on, say, an argument with a partner, a spouse, a child, or a colleague, or the hormonal changes that occur during stages of transition, such as between early childhood and adolescence or between early adulthood and what is politely referred to as "middle age."

As one woman I recently met confessed, "Since I started going through 'the change' my moods are completely unpredictable. One minute I can be completely open and happy; the next, I become a total bitch. I hate everyone and everything. I can argue against anything, and my reasoning seems totally logical to me. Sometimes I'm angry for no reason. On top of that, I'm cold for a minute, and then I'm sweating. I have to turn on the air conditioner in the middle of winter, which drives my husband crazy and only makes me hate him more sometimes.

"I shout at him, 'I'm changing,' but he doesn't seem to get the message. And he won't admit that he's going through a change of sorts himself. He gets tired more quickly. He's irritable. He's gaining weight. Sometimes I wish he could feel 'the change' as dramatically as I do. But then I think I'm glad he doesn't, because otherwise he'd be impossible to live with."

Now, a woman of a certain age may be able to comprehend the changes in her physical being and the effects of such changes on her relationships and realize that such changes are a natural, if uncomfortable, part of a biochemical process. Someone with a little understanding of the ways of the material universe may understand that the atoms and molecules that make up the objects in our lives are also changing, often subtly but sometimes rather obviously, as when a crack appears in a wall or ceiling, or when paint begins peeling. A businessperson may understand that the challenges he deals with on any given day may have something to do with the challenges that the person across the table is facing.

In addition, at some point in early childhood we come to realize that some things, some experiences come to an end. Toys get lost or permanently broken. Parents get divorced. Pets, and of course people, die. Loss, on many levels, is particularly difficult to process, intellectually and emotionally.

There's an old Buddhist story about a woman whose young son had died. She refused to believe that her child was dead, however, and ran from house to house in the village asking for medicine to revive him. Of course, no one could help her. The boy was dead, they pointed out, trying to help her accept the situation. One person, however, recognizing that her mind was disturbed by grief, advised her to seek the Buddha, who was staying in a monastery nearby.

Grasping her child's body closely to her chest, she ran to where the Buddha was staying and asked him for medicine to help her child. The Buddha was in the middle of giving a teaching in front of a large number of people, but the woman pushed through, and seeing her distress, the Buddha answered her request.

"Go back to your village," he told her gently, "and bring me back a few mustard seeds from a house where no one has ever died."

She ran back to her village and began asking each of her neighbors for mustard seeds. Her neighbors were happy to give them to her, but then she had to ask, "Has anyone died here?" They looked at her strangely. Some of them just nodded; others told her yes; and others told her when and under what circumstances a family member's death had occurred.

By the time she completed her circuit of the village, she came to understand through an experience that cut deeper than words that she was not the only person in the world who had suffered a terrible personal loss. Change, loss, and grief were common to all.

Though still grief-stricken by the death of her son, she recognized that she was not alone and her heart cracked open. After the funeral ceremonies for her son were completed, she joined the Buddha and the disciples around him and devoted her life to assisting others in achieving the same degree of recognition.

Now, this woman was an adult. To a child, however, shifts in conditions resulting from interdependence and impermanence present a frightening dilemma. The simplest means of coping with it is to develop what feels like a solid sense of self and an understanding of others that is equally firm and that evolves, in most cases, so slowly and subtly that it's almost unrecognizable.

"SOLID I," "SOLID OTHER"

The open, intelligent level of being known as the "mere I" is highly impressionable and very sensitive to whatever passes through its experience—not all of which is comfortable or pleasant. It is most susceptible to the sense of *difference*, the distinction between self and other, subject and object.

The distinguishing process usually evolves when we're quite young. It develops spontaneously as we explore our world, bumping into things literally and figuratively: when we trip and fall, when we're startled by noises, when we recognize a sustained sense of loneliness or fear if parents or other caregivers aren't around.

We're aided in this process by the adults around us, who with all good intentions start teaching us at a very young age to make distinctions. "This is Grandma," our parents tell us, for example, pointing to the stranger in the room. "Can you smile for Grandma?" Or perhaps, "This is a spoon. Can you say *spoon*?" And we, as parents, are thrilled when our child smiles for Grandma or makes some effort to pronounce the word *spoon*.

There's nothing inherently faulty in this phase of our development as children or the energy expended by our parents and other adults around us on teaching us to make distinctions. After all, we live in a world full of whizzing cars, sharp knives, and strangers who don't have our best interests at heart. We need to learn the difference between a knife and a spoon, between Grandma and a stranger who looks like Grandma. We need some frame of reference, some way to steer through and relate to a wide variety of experiences.

As we begin to emerge from the fluid "mere I" experience into a realm of distinctions, though, we begin to accept such distinctions as solid, true, or real. And that is a point at which we enter a bit of confusion, because nothing in our experience—spoons, Grandma, even our "selves"—are as solid, true, or real as we imagine they are.

Gradually, as we shift out of the fluid movie experience in which we've been immersed—as the people, places, and things around us take on more distinctive shape—we start seeking some sort of stability, something readily definable or dependable, a place where we can rest. We tend to "reify" our experiences—of ourselves, our feelings, our thoughts—to endow them with the solidity of "things."

Out of the reification process emerges what is known in Tibetan as the *dak tenpar dzin*—or *dak dzin* for short. As mentioned earlier, *dak* is the Tibetan word for "self," *tenpar* means "as true," and *dzin* is a form of the verb meaning "to grasp" or "to fixate." We're literally looking for some sense of "I"-ness to hold on to as a solid center in the midst of the unfolding drama of experience.

The seeds of future difficulties are sown, however, if this transition period from the fluidity of the "mere I" to the "solid I" is not handled delicately. If the basic elements of our nature—openness, clarity, and love—aren't nurtured, then we're likely to become frozen. Think of water being turned into ice cubes. Its basic nature as water hasn't changed, but now it's more rigid, separated into little chunks of subjects and objects, good things and bad things, things we want and things we don't want.

In the beginning, the "solid I" is pretty much identified with our bodies. But as we mature, this "solid I" becomes more abstract or conceptual. It evolves into a sense of separate "I"-ness located vaguely inside our bodies or maybe in our imaginations. As we apply tighter, harder labels to our experiences, our thoughts, our emotions, our physical sensations develop a kind of weighty, "thing-like" quality. We begin to identify with our thoughts and feelings as dimensions of experience that are inherently parts of ourselves. As the sense of "I" becomes more solid, the effects of such identification become more powerful and complicated.

At the same time that we assign seemingly true or solid qualities to our selves, a corresponding process begins to evolve through which we begin to assign those same aspects to what or whoever is "not I," or "other." We begin to perceive and to catalog our experiences in terms of friends and enemies; into "things" that we have and "things" that we don't have: "things" that we want and "things" that we don't want.

At this stage in our development, we begin to experience a kind of tension. We begin to identify ourselves in terms of winners or losers, "haves" or "have-nots." The openness, intelligence, and love through which we conduct our relationships become conditional. We begin to look at others in terms of how they can help us or harm us. We begin to develop stories about ourselves and the people we deal with, which determine the choices we make in our everyday experiences, as well as the consequences.

THE "PRECIOUS I"

Our attempts to identify with and as a "solid I" provide the foundation for the third layer of identification, which, in many ways, inhibits us from realizing our potential. In Tibetan, this layer is called the *dak ché dzin*, which literally translates as "grasping the self as precious." The term is often translated as the "self-cherishing I." Unfortunately, while both translations may be technically correct, they don't convey the deep understanding of this layer of identity.

Dak ché dzin really points to a terrible and terrifying sense of the consequences of the ice-cube-separateness established on the level of the "solid I," which drives us to focus on "*my* needs," "*my* wants," "*my* problems," "*my* story" over and above the needs, wants, and problems of others. Our "I" becomes "precious" or "cherished" in the sense that it becomes the main channel through which all our thoughts, feelings, and actions are directed.

This feeling of separateness urges us in two related but seemingly conflicting directions. The first is an urge to protect our ideas about ourselves, even when they're unflattering or destructive to ourselves or others.

For example, as one woman recently confided, "Years ago, I was taken by my mother for an annual checkup with a pediatrician. I was at that time a bit over the weight range considered 'normal' for a girl of that age. The doctor made an offhand remark to my mother, which he probably meant as a joke: 'Better not let her get too close to the stove, or she might melt.'

"I was horrified, but my mother laughed—giggled, really, in an embarrassed way—perhaps because she thought that my size was somehow her fault, a flaw in raising her daughter. Maybe it was an attempt to correct that flaw that often when she saw me walking around the house she'd mutter an unkind jingle: 'Must be jelly, 'cause jam don't shake like that.' Sometimes she'd look at me and tell me I looked like a 'stuffed sausage.'

"Now, over the past few years I've engaged in a diet and exercise program and have lost nearly fifty pounds. My mother is deceased, so she isn't around to make remarks, and I know that the 'jingles' I repeat are fabrications of my own mind.

"But I look in the mirror and I see 'jelly.' I see a 'stuffed sausage.' My friends and family tell me how great I look and how proud of me they are, but in the back of my mind I think I hear them thinking, 'But you could do more. . . .' And I still see 'jelly' and 'sausage' when I look in the mirror. I still see a fat girl who might melt if she gets too close to the stove."

That doesn't sound especially "precious" or "cherishing" does it?

Which brings us to the deeper meaning of the term *cherishing*, which, on a subtle level, refers to holding on to something long past its need or usefulness.

When we "cherish" the "I" or hold on to it as precious, we're holding on to an image that no longer applies, that is no longer useful, and that is in some cases frankly unhealthy.

Why do we do that?

As the conditional relationships based on solid images of ourselves and others evolve, we begin to feel a sense of loneliness or incompleteness. At some level, we know that we've lost an essential connectedness, not only to our own heart but to the hearts of all beings with whom we share this precious planet. We create stories about how and why this disconnect has occurred. These stories become a part of our "solid" identity. They are the basis through which we justify our understanding of ourselves and of the ways in which we understand and respond to others.

No matter how uncomfortable these ideas or stories about ourselves are, they're familiar. There's a saying I've heard among Western students that "familiarity breeds contempt." I don't know if that translates as neatly in other languages, but the basic meaning is that if you experience something often and consistently enough, you cease to take it seriously and begin to feel disrespect toward that experience. From what I've seen and learned over the years, however, it seems more likely that familiarity breeds *content*: that the more often someone experiences something, the more apt, over time, he or she will be to accept it as a normal, natural aspect of life.

This "contented familiarity" is especially obvious among people I've spoken with who became addicted to alcohol or drugs. Even in the midst of their addictions, they knew that these substances were killing them, destroying their livelihoods and families, but the comfort they experienced while engaging in behavior that harmed themselves and others outweighed the damage they were doing and reinforced the feeling that they needed to engage in harmful behavior, even as it was destroying their lives.

"I felt loved," someone recently told me. "I felt powerful. I felt capable of anything. I could talk to people. It was only later that I learned that most of the people I met only barely tolerated me. They could smell the stink on my breath. They'd nod politely and get away as quickly as possible. I didn't notice. All I felt in those times was the comfort, the security, the power. . . ."

Which brings us to the other aspect of the "precious I"—the willingness to seek fulfillment from or confirmation of or identity in someone or something outside of ourselves, in anything that will help us preserve a sense of stability in the face of circumstances that are always changing.

So maybe a better understanding of the "precious I" or "self-cherishing I" would be the "addictive I"—that aspect of self that becomes attached to and feels a need for something beyond the basic spark of warmth, openness, and curiosity to experience a sense of connectedness, of familiarity, of comfort.

We can see that most easily in the area of romantic relationships. We might meet a person and think, "Wow, this person is great! Perfect! Everything I've ever dreamed of!" Maybe we start going out on a few dates, and every time we're together it's like the whole space around us is filled with rainbows. We couldn't be happier. But after a while, maybe we find some little areas of disagreement, edges of our personalities that don't quite fit. Maybe we fight. Then we make up, and then fight again. We blame the other person for being grumpy or loud or not understanding us. Or maybe we blame ourselves for not being attractive enough or understanding enough. The relationship eventually ends, and we're back to feeling incomplete, and we start looking somewhere else, for someone else or something else to heal and complete us, to confirm our sense of solidity.

Sometimes, too, the need to confirm our sense of solidity can be seen in our drive to collect "things," and I'm as guilty of that as anyone else.

A few years ago I was experiencing what some people might call a "midlife crisis." I was sitting in a hotel room in Delhi, waiting to take a flight to Paris, and I saw an advertisement that fascinated me. It featured a young man with a muscular "six-pack" belly (I have a "one-pack," a large roll that spills over my belt). The six-pack guy was standing next to a very attractive young lady with flowing hair and a huge smile that showed an almost scary number of perfect white teeth. Between them they were holding a particular brand of laptop computer. It seemed pretty clear that the ad was trying to say that if you bought this computer, you, too, could have a six-pack belly and a girlfriend with flowing hair and extremely white teeth.

I wasn't immediately impressed.

When I arrived in Paris, I saw a billboard showing the same six-pack guy and the lady with the flowing hair and shiny teeth, holding the same brand of laptop.

From Paris I flew to a teaching engagement in Singapore and saw the same billboard. Then I flew to the United States, and on my way from the airport I saw the same billboard.

I admit that after seeing the same happy people holding the same laptop, I bought it. I thought it would help me be more successful in communicating to the world from the various places I travel throughout the year. I was, I'm a little ashamed to admit, swayed by how happy the people in the advertisement looked. I didn't really think that buying the laptop would transform my "one-pack" to a "six-pack"—but in the back of my mind there was a little thought: "Hey, you never know."

Unfortunately, nowhere in the laptop's instruction manual or the manufacturer's guarantee was there ever a warning that the dust and grit of Tibet would cause the computer to fail. And it did fail. Two weeks after I brought it to Tibet, it just stopped working. After I returned home to Nepal from Tibet I got another laptop.

I don't fault the manufacturers for their inability to build computers that can withstand the rigors of a harsh climate. Like almost everyone else in the world, I'd become an "addicted I." I believed that a product, a "thing," could fill the nervous, insecure space in myself and make me feel happy and fulfilled.

It was a great lesson, though: Even *tulkus* are human. Oh, we might learn a lot of texts and philosophies and benefit from the lessons that women and men have handed down through the ages, but we're as susceptible as anyone else to the various types of temptation that everyone else feels.

Maybe the only advantage a *tulku* has over other people is that we're trained from a very early age to do the best we can to help others break through whatever ideas they learn and lead them to rediscover the spark with which they are born. We're trained to love every living creature until he or she can love themselves. Until every person on earth ceases to view one another as a threat or an enemy; until every person, in every job, every relationship, every encounter, can see the wonder, the beauty, and the potential in everyone with whom they come in contact. Until we show people how to let go of their stories, then fill within themselves the sense of disconnectedness, our job is not done.

It's not a job I could have wished for, but it's the job I was given and ultimately chose to pursue, though in my own way, informed by my experiences as a husband and father, as well as by another layer of "I" that took me quite a while to understand.

THE "SOCIAL I"

One of the ways we look for fulfillment or confirmation is in the eyes of other people. We look to other people for confirmation of who are, who we would like to be, or what we believe about ourselves.

This is a layer that I refer to as the "social I," that aspect or layer of self we develop when dealing with other people. Unlike the other layers of self, the "social I" is not a part of the traditional Buddhist model of "I" or ego layers. My understanding is grounded in my own experience as well as in conversations with Western psychologists, and it's taken me a number of years to identify and describe it.

My confrontation with the "social I" began after I arrived at Tashi Jong monastery to begin my training.

In order to understand the type of training a *tulku* undergoes, I ask you to imagine the very best and the very worst of what might be referred to in some countries as a private school system and in others as the public school system. You're given the opportunity to study with great teachers. In addition to spelling, grammar, vocabulary, history, astronomy, and calligraphy, you're offered a rigorous course in the philosophical foundations of Buddhism, studying the words not only of the Buddha but of all the great Indian and Tibetan masters who followed him. You learn not only the value of empathy, tolerance, patience, and generosity but also practical methods for cultivating such qualities. You learn a wide range of meditation techniques and the rituals associated with the Tibetan form of Buddhism.

Most of the early years of *tulku* training, however, involve rote memorization of texts and ritual movements, so that the *tulku* can complete a teaching or a ceremony when the electricity goes out and everyone is plunged into darkness (not an uncommon occurrence in places like

India and Nepal). You memorize a certain number of pages—maybe two hundred per year—and then you're tested on how well you've memorized the pages. You're given three chances to pass the test. If you fail the third test, it's back to the books.

At the same time, you're indoctrinated into the sense that it's your *duty* not only to master the philosophies and practices but also to preserve a culture on the brink of extinction. The wisdom of men and women accumulated over more than two thousand years will be lost if you don't pay strict attention. If you don't sit, stand, speak, and wear your uniform—the red and yellow robes of a Tibetan Buddhist monastic—perfectly, you're a failure in terms of a noble tradition. You're a failure to your teachers, to your families, and to an infinite number of beings residing in an infinite number of universes who are depending on *you* to carry out your traditional role: a rather heavy responsibility to be placed on the shoulders of a twelve-year-old boy.

I'd arrived at Tashi Jong later than most of the other *tulkus*, who had begun their training at about the age of eight or nine, so I felt hard-pressed to make up for lost time. I suppose, like many children, I wanted to please my teachers, so I applied myself vigorously to my studies and tried my very best to emulate the behavior of my "pre-incarnation." If I pleased my teachers, they were happy; and when they were happy, I was happy. I liked it that they were pleased with my discipline, that they would point me out to others as a model, saying, "Look at Tsoknyi Rinpoche. What a good *tulku* he is. Follow his example." Pleasing my teachers became a sort of addiction, a susceptibility to the conditional sort of love described earlier.

Yet from time to time, I felt a nagging discontent: a sense that I wasn't the reincarnation of some old man and that in pleasing my teachers by acting like one, I was, in a sense, suppressing the basic openness and warmth of my child self: the boy who liked to play, to talk, to laugh, to joke, to move around, to jump across rivers and sometimes land in the water. I was, very gradually, losing the connection to the deep sense of spontaneity, warmth, and playfulness I'd felt for most of my young life. The praise felt good, but not the behavior that generated the praise. A part of me knew I was pretending, and yet I kept on pretending because I liked the praise.

After a year or so, however, even the praise lost a bit of its luster. I knew that I was pretending, behaving in a way that wasn't consistent with how I really felt deep down. I started to feel as if I were living two lives at the same time: the well-behaved, industrious *tulku* and the adolescent boy who didn't like sitting as still as a statue, who wanted to joke around, wander through the village, and make friends with children his own age. Outwardly, I was a model of discipline; inside, my mind was flitting about and my body was raging with adolescent hormones.

That's the trap of the social "I." It's almost set up for conflict because what we're feeling inside may not be what we're trained to project outside. If I behaved exactly like a *tulku* ought to behave, there was no problem. But I couldn't follow the "*tulku* rules" all the time. It wasn't in my nature. I was a social, playful boy. I liked talking to girls, making jokes, relaxing, not being so formal all the time. Consequently I developed a bit of resentment—and then felt guilty about the resentment.

But the anxiety to please, the resentment I felt, and the guilt about the resentment were all wrapped together. And as I grew older I began to ask "Why?"

SEEDS

While the various layers of "I" appear to develop in separate stages according to time and circumstance, these layers actually evolve and support one another in a continuous process. The "mere I," to use an analogy, is a like a seed, within which is contained the potential for the development of the "solid I," which, given a certain combination of conditions, might develop roots underground and a sprout aboveground that develops into a stem, leaves, and some sort of blossoms or fruit that carry the potential for creating new seeds.

This analogy isn't perfect, of course. Some plants only last a season, while others continue to regenerate year after year. Maybe a better analogy would be the combination of wind and weather that bring about what has been called at times a "perfect storm." At other times, conditions come together to produce a "perfect rainbow," such as the double rainbow after recent stormy weather seen, for example, in Southern California.

When we look deeply into the nature of experience, though, we discover that it can't really be named or described, or that the names we use fall somewhat short of the actual experience. While the seed of our personalities may lie in the fluidity of the "mere I," the heart of that seed is emptiness, the great and awesome capacity to experience anything and to be aware of what we're experiencing. We feel something or think something, and we realize, "Hey, something's going on here."

How we define that *something* often depends on the circumstances in which we've been raised and the challenges we've met. But among the thousands of circumstances we encounter as we travel through life, we can be sure of two things: first, that we'll develop an "I" to deal with these circumstances; and second, that the "I"—the ego, or the self (whatever you want to name it)—has gotten a lot of what you might call "bad press" in recent years.

THE "USEFUL I"

Myths grow up around social movements—and that is, in essence, what Buddhism is: a movement. The Buddha urged us to get off our chairs, our couches, and our cushions and get moving; to start living as though our lives meant something; to "awaken" to the knowledge that the ways we think, feel, and act have an effect on the world around us. A lot of people think that Buddhism promotes the idea of extinguishing the idea of "I" or "self" or "ego" altogether. But the idea of extinguishing "ego" or "self" or "I" is inaccurate. You may as well try to "extinguish" your feet or your hands.

Hands and feet are useful. They help us to type, to drive, to walk, to reach in our pockets to produce money for food. And unless through accident or tragedy we lose them, we take our hands and feet for granted.

Among his many teachings, the Buddha urged not to take our "I's" for granted. A lot of what we've learned about "I" through life experience, for example, can be quite valuable. There are times, for example, when the "social I" is quite useful. Many people throughout history used their "social I's," reaching out to others through a charismatic public persona to endorse a more open and compassionate approach to living. Many doctors, nurses, teachers, corporate workers, and other unsung heroes around the world use their "social I's," their "solid I's," and even the stories wrapped up in their "precious I's" as a means of getting through the day. But they're not used *by* them. Once out of public view, many of the heroes of our world let go of their social identities, their stories, even their attachment to their true or solid selves, and drop gently and gratefully back into the openness, warmth, and fluidity of the "mere I."

The challenge the Buddha proposed was to learn to rest in openness of the "mere I" even while using the various other "I's"; to maintain a sense of warmth and openness even when, for instance, facing someone who disagrees with you.

Think of developing this capacity to use your "I's" as something like brushing your teeth. We need to eat and drink in order to survive. But food and beverages often leave some sort of a residue on the teeth. So rather than just stop eating or drinking, we brush our teeth. If we didn't brush our teeth, the residue from food and drink would build up and our teeth would rot. So we have to engage in both activities: sustaining ourselves with food and drink, and caring for our teeth.

Similarly, we don't need to get rid of the various "I's." We just need to brush away the residue we pick up along the way.

As we contemplate the enormous variety of factors that must come together to produce a specific sense of self, the residue attached to the various layers of "I" can spontaneously begin to loosen and then dissolve. We become more willing to let go of the desire to control or block our thoughts, emotions, sensations, and so on and begin to experience them without pain or guilt, absorbing their passage simply as manifestations of a universe of infinite possibilities.

In so doing, we begin to reconnect with the basic spark of our being. Essence love begins to shine more brightly, and our hearts open up to others. We become better listeners, more fully aware of everything going on around us, and more able to respond spontaneously and appropriately to situations that used to trouble or confuse us. Slowly, perhaps on a level so subtle we might not even notice it's happening, we find ourselves awakening to a free, clear, loving state of mind.

But it takes practice to learn how to distinguish between what is residue and what is useful. It takes practice to learn how to live comfortably and openly as embodied beings and face the challenges that accompany that state. It takes practice to deal with other embodied beings, who may not have had the knowledge or the opportunity to reconnect with their basic spark, or even know that it abides within them.

And so, over the next few chapters, we'll focus on those practices, some of which you may find easy to understand and engage in from the very beginning, others of which may require a little time and patience. Don't be discouraged if you find yourself in such a situation. These practices have been developed and refined over centuries by masters who spent many years bringing them to fruition. Be kind to yourself as you proceed along this journey. This kindness, in itself, is a means of awakening the spark of love within you and helping others to discover that spark within themselves.

There's an old Tibetan saying: "If you walk with haste, you won't reach Lhasa. Walk gently and you'll reach your goal." This saying comes from the days when people in eastern Tibet would make a pilgrimage to Lhasa, the capital city, in the central region of the country. Pilgrims who wanted to get there quickly would walk as fast as they could, but because of the pace they set for themselves, they'd get tired or sick and have to return home. Those who traveled at an easy pace, pitched camp for the night, enjoyed one another's company, and then continued on the next day, actually arrived at Lhasa more quickly.

FIVE

Method

It's one thing to understand certain things about our nature, and another to do something with that understanding.

To use a small example, during the years I spent at Tashi Jong, I lived quite sparingly on a monastic diet. I was, like so many students there, quite thin. When I returned to Nepal at twenty-one, after I'd completed my training at Tashi Jong, my diet changed considerably. Suddenly there was Coca-Cola! And so much rice, a staple of the Nepali diet. I gorged on both; such delight!

About a year after I returned to Nepal, a friend from Tashi Jong came to visit me. "Rinpoche," he exclaimed, "you've grown."

Very quickly I realized that he didn't mean that I'd grown taller but wider.

"What are you eating?" he asked.

I told him that I was drinking about six or seven bottles of Coca-Cola a day and eating a lot of rice.

He was horrified.

"You've got to stop," he warned. "That diet will kill you!"

He explained a lot about the effects of the sugar in the beverages I was drinking and the carbohydrates in the rice I was eating. I didn't understand everything he was saying, but the seriousness in his expression and in the tone of his voice convinced me that I had to make some changes in my life, that I had to act.

I found it fairly easy to cut down on rice, because I wasn't really attached to it as part of my diet. It took me seven years to cut out Coca-Cola, however. Although it was only a recent addition to my diet, it was one I enjoyed so much that I'd formed an attachment to it; it had become part of my new identity as a non-monk, so to speak. Seven years is a relatively short time, though, so I can sympathize with people who find it difficult to deal with patterns and attachments formed at a much earlier age and have continued for a much longer period.

In other words, it's one thing to give up Coca-Cola. It's quite another to begin to let go of who you think you are.

Fortunately, the Buddha and the great teachers who followed in his footsteps proposed a variety of methods to deal with that particular challenge.

MINDFULNESS

One of the most effective of these methods is *mindfulness*—a practice, or rather a set of practices, designed to assist us in uncovering or unfreezing the various layers of "I" that prevent us from experiencing the basic spark that lies at the heart of our being.

Mindfulness has been described and explained by many people who are wiser than I. My understanding is perhaps a little plainer than others might offer, but it is grounded in my own experience and in the experience of many of the students I've met over the years.

And like many Buddhist teachings, whatever I can offer in the way of clarification involves a bit of a story—because in order to understand mindfulness, you have to have some bit of the mind itself, a conversation among scientists and scholars that has gone on for quite a while and will probably continue for many years to come.

MIND

Years ago, when one of the greatest twentieth-century masters of Tibetan Buddhism, Dilgo Khyentse Rinpoche—a large man with an extraordinarily serene grace and one of the gentlest voices I've ever heard—came to Tashi Jong, my tutor rounded us up and practically chased us toward the place where Rinpoche was teaching. I was only thirteen years old at the time, and after more than thirty years it's hard for me to remember half the things he said. A few stuck with me, however.

"What is the mind?" he asked. "Where is it? Does it have a color? A size? A shape? A location?"

Now these might not be questions that consume the attention of a thirteen-year-old boy, at least not articulated in the way Rinpoche asked them. But I suppose, even at thirteen, some of us begin to wonder why we think the things we think, why we feel the way we feel—what, to use an American expression, makes us "tick."

So now I have to confess another bit of disobedience I engaged in while at Tashi Jong.

To try and figure out the answers to Dilgo Khyentse Rinpoche's questions, I started "borrowing" books from the monastery library that weren't really authorized for students of my age. Not entire books—Tibetan books are for the most part made up of unbound pages grouped in collections known in Tibetan as *pechas*—and I did return these pages, more or less quickly, to the library after I'd finished reading them.

One of the sets of pages I borrowed was by a great Tibetan Buddhist teacher of the nineteenth century, Patrul Rinpoche, who is respected by all schools of Tibetan Buddhism. His masterwork, *The Words of My Perfect Teacher*, is one of the clearest guides to realizing our potential as human beings.

The pages I borrowed were not from that book, however, but from a smaller, lesser-known work about meditation. A particular sentence in these pages struck me deeply, triggering what you might call a "lightning recognition," an experience in which, on an emotional, intellectual, and even sensory level, we just "get" what people are talking about. Roughly translated, this short sentence went like this: "That which seeks the mind *is* the mind."

It took me a few years to capture this lightning recognition in words that might be understood by others. In the simplest terms possible, what we call the "mind" is not a thing but a perpetually moving event, operating on different but related levels. One level, normal—or everyday—awareness, focuses on the types of relative experience we have when driving cars; managing relationships with partners, spouses, children, and coworkers; and navigating the difficult choices in a world troubled by social, political, and economic challenges. This relative awareness, or relative mind, tends to run around in circles, repeating the same messages.

The other, more expansive level is an awareness of our relative awareness, identical with the fundamental openness and clarity described earlier.

These two aspects of mind are connected, not unlike siblings reaching out toward each other. Relative mind, in moments of great challenge, seeks guidance and assistance from a broader, more open awareness that "sees" solutions that our everyday consciousness may not be able to discern.

On some level, our everyday, or relative mind might not perceive the possibilities available to cope with day-to-day challenges. But, sometimes dimly, sometimes brightly, it recognizes the possibility of a more open, wiser, and warmer awareness, and, however reluctantly, seeks it.

We become aware of this awareness through the practice of mindfulness.

AWARE AND ATTENTIVE

The term *mindfulness* is often considered a translation of the Tibetan term *drenpa*, "to become aware of an object, a condition, or a situation." More precisely, *drenpa* is the aspect of consciousness that draws attention to an object. But merely being aware is not really the entire practice of mindfulness.

Often we become aware of whatever it is that grabs our attention; sometimes, the thoughts and feelings of which we become conscious are so uncomfortable we push them into the background of all the stuff we have to deal with in the course of daily life. We're "mindful" in this way a lot of the time. For example, when we gnaw at a particular challenge, like how to feed our families, pay our bills, or deal with a romantic relationship that has grown sour. This type of awareness, which might be called "everyday mindfulness," is actually only the first half of mindfulness practice.

It's not enough to be aware. We also have to be alert. We have to ask ourselves, when we experience discomfort, trouble, or pain, "What's going on here?"

This aspect of mindfulness is known in Tibetan as *shezhin*, which may best be translated as "knowing one's own awareness." *Shezhin* is really the heart of mindfulness, the attentive aspect of consciousness through which we observe the mind itself in the act of being aware of an object. While many of us may focus on our thoughts, emotions, sensations, and so on as we multitask throughout our day, we're rarely *attentive* to the mind that is aware of these experiences.

For example, on my first trip to America, back in the 1990s, some friends took me to dinner at very fancy hotel in San Francisco. I entered the restaurant wearing my robes—which in Nepal or India would have drawn some curious stares. Monks and lamas don't usually go out to restaurants for dinner. It's not forbidden, exactly, but it isn't seen as "proper."

In San Francisco, the waiters and waitresses were very attentive. They seated us, took our meal requests, and then disappeared—quite a departure from what I'd experienced in some other countries, where you either couldn't find a waiter or waitress to save your life or had to cope with someone standing at the table staring, waiting to fulfill your every need before you're even aware that you needed something.

When I went to the restaurant in San Francisco, I was a little anxious that people would stare at me, dressed in my robes, thinking I was some sort of alien. To my surprise, though, they didn't show any special interest. They welcomed us, seated us, and took our food orders. The food arrived in a timely manner, and the waiters went away. When I found I needed something—more water, for instance, or a condiment (I admit, I'm attached to hot peppers)—and started searching for something on the table, within a few seconds a waitress appeared, asking, "Sir, is there something you need?" I told her what I needed, she provided it, and then she was gone.

The waitresses and waiters weren't standing around staring—but they were alert and aware; they had *drenpa* and *shezhin* together.

I watched them, too, while they were carrying food to different tables. Every one of them was attentive to the space around them, to the plates or trays that they were carrying, to the others with whom they were working and the people they were serving. They were, in other words, pretty much perfect practitioners of mindfulness: aware of their surroundings and alert to the demands of their jobs. I'll bet that few of them would say they were Buddhists. But they were practicing some of the basic principles of Buddhism, exhibiting awareness of their surroundings and a sympathetic alertness to the needs of others around them. They were conscious in a very specific way.

THE MIND AND CONSCIOUSNESS

In the Buddhist tradition there are actually eight different types of consciousness. Sounds like a lot, I know. We tend to think in a rather vague and uncertain way. But Buddhist masters of the past, like scientists of contemporary times, were determined to understand how we perceive and respond to the world around us, as well as to experiences we undergo internally. After lengthy investigation and debate they determined eight pathways or types of consciousness through which we receive, process, and interpret experience.

The first five are known as the *sensory consciousnesses*. In modern terms, we'd probably just refer to them as the senses: sight, smell, hearing, taste, and touch. But the Buddhist masters, like contemporary scientists, sought to emphasize the *process* through which different sense organs recognized, distinguished, and relayed messages about their experiences to higher levels of awareness and interpretation. Each of the five sensory consciousnesses, in its particular way, is aware that *something* is going on. The eyes are "conscious" of what they see when they become aware of seeing something, the ears are "conscious" of what they hear when they become aware of hearing something, and so on.

Each of these sensory consciousnesses sends messages "higher up"—and that's where things get interesting.

The messages sent by the five sensory consciousnesses are received by what is known as a *sixth consciousness*—not to be confused with a "sixth sense." It's easier to think of the sixth consciousness as a receiver of information, rather like a telephone operator. It doesn't judge or interpret the messages passed on to it. Its function is mainly to tell the conscious mind that *something* is happening: "Hey, a smell is going on here." "Hey, a sound is going on here."

Interpreting that smell, that sound, and so on as good or bad, pleasant or unpleasant, and so on, is—as I was taught—the function of the *seventh consciousness*, which is in many ways shaped by social, cultural, and personal influences, in a similar fashion to the ways in which we modify computer programs and adopt or reject options available on social networking sites.

The *eighth consciousness* is a kind of storehouse of all the patterns and programs ever "installed" on our living systems, and a complete record of any and all modifications we've made under societal or personal pressure. The eighth consciousness stores every aspect of all of our experience—every idea, every emotional pattern, every sense memory—kind of like the hard drive on a computer.

THE PURPOSE OF MINDFULNESS

One of the purposes of mindfulness practice is to stabilize consciousness at the sixth level, simply noticing without judgment or interpretation. We might call this an innocent or authentic awareness, which helps us to unravel the patterns made up of sensory perceptions, memories, thoughts, and feelings, and to begin to reconnect with the basic spark.

For instance, I met a woman a while ago who had gone through a very painful divorce after discovering that her husband had been having an affair with a woman who wore a particular brand of perfume. For years after the divorce, every time she smelled that perfume—whether going through a department store, in an elevator, or on a coworker—she had a terrifically negative reaction. But the perfume itself was not intrinsically negative.

Of course, this is a simple example. One can live without a certain brand of perfume, or exposure to it can be very brief. But we may experience other conditions that are unavoidable—for instance, being among crowds of people or having to speak in front of a group—which can trigger more complicated, challenging reactions.

When we stabilize consciousness on the sixth level, we allow ourselves a little bit of a pause before the interpretations on the seventh level begin to kick in, so to speak. And that little pause can make a big difference in how we interpret our experience.

WAKING THE HEART

As I began to travel around the world teaching, I heard a lot about mindfulness from a number of people. It seemed to me that many people had begun to describe mindfulness as a type of mental or emotional calming exercise aimed at soothing a personal restlessness and unease. I heard about all these sorts of applications—mindfulness of eating, mindfulness of talking, mindfulness of walking, and so on. Such practices seemed to be very useful in some way in helping people slow down and focus, but I couldn't reconcile these practices with the deeper meaning of mindfulness about which I'd been taught.

In the Tibetan tradition, you see, we don't teach mindfulness as a practice of simply moving slowly—for example, drinking tea mindfully: Now the hand is moving very slowly toward the cup, touching the cup, raising it to the mouth, tasting the tea, focusing very slowly on swallowing, and setting the cup back down.

When I returned to Asia, I told one of my teachers, Adeu Rinpoche, about my experiences and asked his advice. Adeu Rinpoche was one of the greatest masters of Tibetan Buddhism who walked this earth in recent years. Caught up in the political and cultural difficulties that wracked Tibet in the latter part of the twentieth century, he was imprisoned for nearly twenty years. Astonishingly, he described those years of his imprisonment as one of the best meditation retreats he'd ever experienced. The labor assigned to him was very hard, but, as he admitted, he was privileged to meet other great teachers who had similarly been caught up in the chaos, and in the quiet of their barracks, he learned a great deal from them.

I was twenty years old when I first met Adeu Rinpoche during my first trip to Tibet, soon after his release from prison. He was a very tall man, with a commanding—you might even call it "regal"—presence, undiminished by years of cleaning prison toilets and other menial tasks. I stayed close to him during that first visit, and during that time I began to see that the power of his presence wasn't based on anything about his voice, height, or other physical characteristics. He emanated a kind of emotional warmth and openness that inspired in everyone around him a deep sense of serenity and safety. Of course, having mastered just about every aspect of Buddhist teaching, he was a brilliant individual; but he was also one of those rare people who, when you were near him, made you feel that you were just as brilliant.

In part, the gift of brilliance he gave to all who approached him came from his willingness to answer questions (and, of course, the accumulation of knowledge of Buddhist teachings and his extraordinary sensitivity to provide answers suited to the temperament of each and every student). He never thought a question was stupid or irrelevant. He never told someone to look in some book or other for an answer.

So a few years after my first teaching tour, I asked him about the types of mindfulness I'd heard about, and he explained to me that what passes for mindfulness practice in many modern cultures were very useful baby steps. So many people, he went on to say, have become used to rushing as a way of life, to getting a lot of things accomplished in a very short time. This habit often results in a disconnection between *what* we're doing and *why* we're doing it, a gulf between our actions and the motivation behind them.

"Always remember," he told me, "that the main goal of any practice is to awaken the heart."

When I asked for further explanation he told me that the ultimate goal of mindfulness is to free all living creatures from their patterns in order to experience the openness, wisdom, and warmth that is the essence of our being and the essence of *bodhicitta*. In order to do that, we have to experience that freedom for ourselves. Baby steps may be useful, but most of the people I'd be teaching weren't babies.

It was time to teach adult steps.

FOUR FOUNDATIONS OF MINDFULNESS

Our minds on the relative level of awareness are pulled in many directions, like a balloon pushed by different flows of air. So when we practice mindfulness, it's important to remember that in the beginning we need to apply a little gentle effort in placing our attention and alertness on a particular area of experience. We can't simply "be mindful"; we need to be mindful *of* something. We need a focus.

Over the course of more than forty years of teaching, the Buddha identified four areas of focus through which we can become more aware and alert, to develop a familiarity with the basic spark of being and allow that spark to gradually develop into *bodhicitta*, the fully awakened heart.

These areas of focus have become known over time as the Four Foundations of Mindfulness, which have been interpreted in many ways by many teachers.

The first three are fairly easy to understand. Mindfulness of Body is the recognition that we live in a body, with all its fruits and fragilities. Mindfulness of Feeling is basically the practice of resting alert awareness on the experience of emotions, without necessarily judging them. Mindfulness of Thought is a similar practice that enables us to be alert and awake to our thoughts as they occur.

The fourth foundation, often literally translated as Mindfulness of Dharma, is a little trickier to explain. *Dharma* is a Sanskrit term that has a variety of meanings, including "law," "rule," "obligation"; or, more generally, "the truth," "the nature of things"; or, more simply, "the way things are." In terms of mindfulness practice—as I was taught, anyway—Dharma, as an object of attention, has more to do with "the way things are" than with any particular laws or obligations.

But we'll get to that later.

As we begin our journey across our particular bridges, it's easiest to begin by bringing our attention, our alertness, our kindness, and our warmth to that aspect of our experience most obviously associated with our sense of "I."

SIX

Minding the Body

I f you're reading this book, chances are good that you are an embodied being. It's surprising how many of us forget that small fact as we
go about our days. It's so easy to get caught up in thoughts and feelings
and overlook this extraordinary system of muscles, bones, organs, and
so on that serves as a physical support for our thoughts, feelings, and
behaviors.

When practicing Mindfulness of Body, we start gently with a simple
appreciation that we *have* a body, a basic ground of experience. The
practice is a bit like mind and body shaking hands: "Mind, this is body.
Body, this is mind. Oh, hello. How do you do?"

We can begin by simply noticing: "There is a leg. There is a toe."
We can simply notice, too, that there is a heart that is beating; there
are lungs that are expanding and contracting; there is blood coursing
through veins. We can also notice physical sensations such as being
cold or being warm, feeling pain in the knees, back, or shoulders, and
so on. The point of the practice of Mindfulness of Body is to simply
allow ourselves to become alert to the physical aspect of our being
in a very easygoing and gentle way, without judging it or identifying
with it.

Just noticing these aspects of our experience can induce a relaxed, grounded state, a sense of simply being of which we are often unaware.

Through the practice of Mindfulness of Body what we're really doing is taking a moment to simply appreciate the fact of being in a body. "This is what it feels like when it's resting . . . this is what it feels like when it's moving . . . this is what it feels like to sit . . . this is what it feels like to stand . . . this is what it feels like to rest my hand on a table." Your mind is really engaged in the here and now, connecting with the bare awareness of having a body at rest or in motion . . . simple facts of being present that many of us haven't thought about in a long, long time. The very fact that we have fingers can become a source of fascination and appreciation when freed from any judgment about whether they're nice fingers, short fingers, or long fingers.

POSTURE

So how do we start minding our bodies?

One way is to begin practice by assuming, if we're able to, a physical posture that is comfortable and stable.

When we first begin to engage in any sort of mindfulness practice, we may find it hard to focus. Our attention jumps around like a nervous rabbit. Much of the restlessness we experience is due simply to inexperience. But we can compensate for that in some way by adopting a gently supportive physical posture that allows us not only to become more alert to our physical bodies but also to focus our attention.

There are two approaches to physical posture: formal and informal. The formal method is described in terms of seven "points" or physical positions.

The first point involves establishing a solid base that anchors you to the environment in which you're practicing. Cross your legs so that each foot rests on the opposite leg. If that's not possible, just cross one foot on top of the opposite leg and rest your other foot beneath the opposite leg. If neither arrangement is comfortable, you can just cross your legs. And if sitting cross-legged on the floor or a cushion—even on your couch or your bed—is painful or not possible, just sit with your feet resting evenly on the floor.

The second point is to rest your hands in your lap, with the back of one hand resting in the palm of the other. It really doesn't matter which hand is placed on top, and you can switch their positions at any time. It's also okay to just lay your hands palms down over your legs. The third point, meanwhile, involves allowing some space between your arms and your upper body, lifting and spreading the arms enable you to breathe as fully and freely as possible.

The fourth point is to keep your spine as straight as possible, what you might call the most important physical expression of alertness. You don't want to tense your spine so much that you find yourself bending backward, but neither do you want to slouch. Think, rather, of building each vertebra, one on top of the other in a nice, straight column.

The fifth point involves letting your head rest evenly on your neck, so that your chin isn't crushing your throat or resting so far back that it crunches the seven little bones at the top of the spine. You want a little "breath" between these bones, and if you allow it, you'll likely experience a sensation of freedom along your whole spine and in other parts of your body.

The sixth point concerns the mouth. If we take a moment to examine the way we hold our mouths, we may discover a habit of keeping our lips, teeth, tongue, and jaws rather rigidly closed. Some of us are so tense in this area that we grind our teeth, press our lips into tight little lines, or develop frown lines. Of course, the sixth point doesn't mean keeping the mouth wide open as if we're swallowing something huge. Rather, it means allowing the mouth to rest naturally as it does when we're at the point of falling asleep, maybe a bit open, maybe totally closed, but not tense either way.

The seventh, and last, point involves the eyes. Many people, when they begin practice, find it easier to experience a sense of focus or steadiness by keeping their eyes closed. This is fine at the beginning. However, I've seen that people who keep their eyes closed tend to drift into such a tranquil state that their attention begins to wander. Some people actually fall asleep. So after a few days of practice, it's better to keep your eyes open, so that you can stay alert and clear. This doesn't mean glaring straight ahead without blinking. Just leave your eyes open as they normally are throughout the day. Remember that the point of mindfulness is to remain alert and aware.

When practicing mindfulness, you can also adopt an informal three-point posture, which can be assumed at times when it may be unsuitable (for example, while driving, cooking, or grocery shopping) or physically impossible to use the formal posture. The three points are simple: Keep your spine as straight as possible, the muscles of your body relaxed, and your feet grounded.

There's a final, often unexpressed, point: Breathe.

Often, especially in challenging moments, we forget to breathe, and when that happens, we become a bit mindless. Our attention tends to become fixed on the challenge at hand. We forget our bodies. We forget our minds. We forget our hearts. We forget any sense of what we're capable of being and become puppets of circumstance.

SCANNING

Assuming a stable and comfortable posture is a good start in terms of aligning the mind and the body. The actual practice involves a few different methods, the first of which is an easy exercise in what may be called "scanning," a very simple handshake between the mind and the body.

Lightly draw your attention to your body from the top of the head to the tip of the toes. Don't focus too intently on any part. Just bring a bare attention to each area.

Sometimes, of course, a physical sensation of discomfort will arise; that's normal. But it's not necessary during this exercise to dwell on such sensations or to go looking for the causes. Instead, just note the experience and move on to the next part of the body—shaking hands, so to speak, with every part: "This is my forehead. How do you do, forehead?" "This is my nose. How do you do, nose?"

For the practice known as mindfulness to have any effect, we need to learn to be polite toward the experiences we discover in the scanning process. Maybe someday politeness will be the word used instead of mindfulness. But before that can occur, we need to reach across the islands of discontent within ourselves and shake hands between our experiences and the stories that surround our experiences.

NOTICING

Scanning is one way to practice. Alternatively, we can just take note of the first thing that catches our awareness when we bring attention to the body: our hand, for example, or our leg, or our foot. For me, the simple act of noticing works very well. I see something and then let my attention take in all the details. Just noticing the details and appreciating the capacity to notice them excites some appreciation, an acknowledgment that I haven't really noticed these things in a long time.

Noticing doesn't imply any sort of extreme effort. We don't have to grow sentimental about noticing the lines on our palms, the wrinkles around our eyes, or the calluses on our feet. Nor do we have to concentrate really forcefully. We just let our minds caress our hands, our feet, our noses.

Try that for a minute or so.

Caress your body with attention.

You might experience some feedback: tales related to the body about it being tired, old, wrinkled, painful, or not working as it should. But this review will confirm that you *have* a body, that you still demonstrate the miracle of being alive.

I've met with people who, for various reasons, have been confined to wheelchairs and in some cases are not able to feel much of their physical bodies. Through the marvels of modern technology, however, they're able to breathe, take nourishment, and communicate with others, and the glow in their eyes inspires me. Throughout their ordeals, they've discovered a sense of triumph in being alive. That's the essence of mindfulness practice. It's about appreciating the fact that we're *alive*. There's a certain joy that arises from this simple recognition—a sense of possibility and a gut-level connection to other beings. Because we're alive, we can make certain choices that affect not only our own lives but the lives of countless others.

Whatever you notice, just rest there for a moment—don't hang on too tightly or work to keep your attention on one form or another; that will occur gradually as your mind becomes accustomed to this approach to attention.

MOVING

Another way to practice Mindfulness of Body, if we're able, is simply to watch our hands move, uncurling or trailing them through space. When we get bored with watching our hands we might shift our attention to something else, like moving our arms or shoulders.

I'm not really good at sitting still. Maybe that's a result of being a parent. Children are always moving, often in ways that make parents a bit nervous. I know that as a child, I definitely didn't make my parents' lives any easier by constantly seeking out adventure.

But mindfulness itself is an adventure, and I actually find it easier to practice Mindfulness of Body while engaging in some sort of movement, simply noticing my physical body as it comes close to other forms in the environment that are present right here, right now. "Okay, my foot is on this part of the floor . . . wow . . . my leg is near the table . . . wow . . . it's near the chair . . ." and so on.

Maintaining focus on the experience of moving develops a sense of simple gratitude toward being able to move at all. You also develop an alertness and awareness of physical space through which the body moves and other forms appear, and you begin to naturally develop a kind of harmony with the environment around you, almost as though you're dancing with physical reality.

Try it for a minute or two.

Sometimes mindfulness on this level can be taken a bit too seriously, however. A while ago, I watched someone walking very slowly and asked him if he was feeling okay. (That's one of the advantages of being a short, nearly bald guy wearing glasses and red robes: You get to ask questions.)

The man replied, "I'm practicing mindful walking."

I didn't feel it was my place to correct him in that moment, but I remembered that at Tashi Jong, there were a lot of people who had spent years sitting in caves, hardly moving at all. But when they came back to the monastery they walked pretty quickly when going about their duties. Their hearts were focused on running the monastery, teaching students, serving people who came for help. They never missed a step and seemed to glide along the paths to different buildings. They were guided by the intention to help others. That's the intention behind mindfulness: to help, to serve, to love.

We can walk slowly or eat slowly if that helps us to be mindful of our bodies. But we mustn't forget the meaning behind our movement: to help, to serve, and to love.

FORM

Mindfulness of Body is sometimes translated as Mindfulness of Form, a practice that extends attention to all types of forms: the furniture and other things we find in a room, on the street, in a restaurant, on a train, and so on. It's essentially practice in grounding ourselves in the relative reality in which we function.

Ordinarily our habit of visual perception is a bit fuzzy. We don't really see the kitchen table very clearly; we don't see our hands very distinctly. They become generalized objects. So in addition to helping to ground us, Mindfulness of Body—or more generally, Mindfulness of Form—also offers us the opportunity to sharpen our perceptual capabilities.

So take maybe a minute or so to focus on a form right now, in whatever place you happen to be. The form doesn't matter. It could be your hand, a table, the book you're holding in one hand or the iPod in the other.

Just notice it. . . .

Just see it. . . .

Okay, the minute is up.

How was that experience?

Did you feel a little more present? A little more grounded? Or maybe a little bit scared?

Any of those reactions are possible when we first begin to relate mindfully to the body and the world of forms. It does take a while to break old habits, after all. That simple willingness to see, to place bare attention on what we see, can be a bit challenging at first. But after a while, such experiments do become easier.

And once we begin, we can extend that attention, that appreciation, to the room, to the world, to the whole universe of form: the trees outside our window, or the grass, or flower beds. Even sitting in a chair in a room, we can begin to appreciate being part of a much larger realm of clear and present forms. And when we get up from our chairs, we can begin to carry that awareness, that alertness, and that appreciation with us.

RECALLING WONDER

As children, we fall in love with the wonder of being alive. Our bodies fascinate us; the things around us fascinate us. In a way, the practice of Mindfulness of Body is a big step in falling back in love with the sheer wonder of being alive. But we can't accomplish that all at once, anymore than we can cross a bridge in a single step. We have to take our experiences a step at a time, learning to walk before we learn to run.

As a parent, of course, I've seen that once my daughters learned to walk, it didn't take much time for them to try to run. All too often they ran into trouble, as most of us do. As children, we may chase a ball into a busy street. As adults we may find ourselves chasing a person who may not have our best interests at heart or chasing a role in society for which we may not be suited.

Mindfulness of Body helps us to respond to the tendency to

run—or at least to question what we're running from or where we're running to. It's the first step in stopping to look at our "I"dentities, to cut through the stories we tell ourselves about ourselves, which in many cases inhibit our tremendous possibilities.

For example, I was recently told about a student who ran into his teacher's room one day in a state of great distress.

"My lower back is all tensed up," he exclaimed, "and I'm so uptight that I'll never be able to relate to other people, I'm always going to be an outsider, I can't communicate."

The teacher looked at him and said, "Your lower back is tense."

"Yes! Yes!" the student shouted. "So I just can't relate to other people. I can't feel compassion. I'm always going to be alone."

The teacher looked at him again, and said, "Your back is tense."

"That's what I said," the student replied anxiously. "So I'm just cut off from other people. This is terrible."

After another minute, the teacher looked at him and said, "Your back is tense. The rest of what you're saying is a story."

But where do such stories live?

SEVEN

The Subtle Body

I was young, still in the early stages of my training, when my primary tutor, Tselwang Rindzin, introduced me to an aspect of being that helped explain to me the unease I'd begun feeling at Tashi Jong.

For several years, I'd experienced stomach and mouth ulcers and sores on my scalp. I couldn't sleep. I couldn't eat. I couldn't decide between doing whatever it took to make the sickness stop or crawling away into a hole to die.

Finally, Tselwang Rindzin began to explain that the difficulties I was experiencing arose from an aspect of being alive that is known in the Buddhist tradition as the subtle body, which may best be understood as the place where emotions emerge and abide, asserting an often tangible effect on the physical body.

It was late afternoon when he sat me down for a talk. The other *tulkus* living in the small hut we shared with him were chatting outside with some of the monks. I could hear their cheery voices as my tutor and I sat on his bed watching the golden sunlight deepen through a small window.

"I've been keeping a close watch on you," he began, "and maybe I've been a little harder on you than on other students because you came here late and the Tsoknyi lineage is so important."

I started to sweat, waiting for what he would say next. I was absolutely sure he was going to give me a scolding. After all, he'd caught me running off to the nearby village to watch movies and heard the stories about how I'd talked to village girls.

"Your studies have gone very well, though," he continued, "and you have a somewhat good intellectual understanding of the self and how that can limit a person's ability to really take the teachings of the Buddha to heart. But . . ."

He paused.

The sun was slowly setting, and I felt a shiver run down my spine.

"I can also see," he eventually continued, "that you're unhappy, and that unhappiness has made you ill and has also caused you to be a little disobedient."

His face was stern as usual, and I waited for the scolding to come.

Instead, after a moment his expression softened a little, and I could see by small signs in the way he shifted his body that he had something else planned.

"So now," he said, "I think it's time to teach you a little something that isn't part of the traditional form of training."

I didn't move a muscle, not wanting to betray my eagerness, as he gave one of his rare smiles.

"You know you have a physical body," he began, "and you've come a long way toward understanding how the mind acts to create a sense of self. But there's a layer of"—he searched for the word—"experience that lies between these two. That layer is what we call the subtle body."

He sighed.

"To describe the subtle body is as hard as trying to describe the taste of water. You know when you're drinking water. You can feel the need of it when you're thirsty. You can feel the relief when your body receives its moisture. But can you actually describe the taste of it to someone else?

"Similarly, can you describe the feeling of emotional balance to someone else, or the relief when you experience it? I don't know," he murmured, "but I'm going to try."

SUBTLE PARTS

According to Tibetan tradition the emotional patterns that dictate our inner sense of balance or imbalance, as well as the physical and emotional manifestations of persistent imbalance, are functions of the subtle body.

The subtle body is very rarely discussed in texts or in public teachings. It's understood to be one of the higher or more advanced teachings of Tibetan Buddhism. However, I believe that understanding the subtle body and its influence on our thoughts, actions, and particularly our emotions is essential to understanding the layers that obscure our ability to relate warmly and openly to ourselves, others, and the conditions that surround our lives. Without understanding the subtle body, moreover, most meditation practices become simply exercises in extending our own comfort zones, a series of techniques that result in preserving the solid sense of "I."

Essentially the subtle body is a kind of interface between the mind and the physical body, a means by which these two aspects of being interact. A simple traditional image involves the relationship between a bell and clapper, the little metal ball that strikes against the sides of the bell. The clapper represents the subtle body, the nexus of feelings, while the bell represents the physical body. When the clapper hits the bell, the physical body—nerves, muscles, and organs—is affected and sound occurs.

The subtle body, however, is a bit more complex than a bell. It's made up of three related features. The first are composed of a collection of what in Tibetan are called *tsa*, usually translated as "channels" or "pathways." People familiar with acupuncture may find a similarity between these channels and the meridians often described in texts about acupuncture. Others might find it easier to recognize a similarity between *tsa* and the network of nerves that extend throughout the body, with which they're actually closely correlated.

The channels are the means through which what we might call "sparks of life" move. In Tibetan, these sparks are called *tigle*, which may be translated as "drops" or "droplets"—an interpretation we're given so that we can form some kind of mental image of what passes through the channels.

Nowadays, of course, we can begin to imagine these "drops" as neurotransmitters, the body's "chemical messengers" that affect our physical, mental, and emotional states. Some of these neurotransmitters are fairly well-known: for example, serotonin, which is influential in depression; dopamine, a chemical associated with the anticipation of pleasure; and epinephrine (more commonly known as adrenaline), a chemical often produced in response to stress, anxiety, and fear. Neurotransmitters are extremely small molecules, and while their effects on our mental and physical states can be quite noticeable, their passage between various organs of the body could still be called subtle.

Tigle are carried through the channels by an energy force known in Tibetan as *lung* (pronounced "loong"), the basic meaning of which is "wind," the force that blows us one way or another, physically, mentally, and emotionally. In the Buddhist tradition, all movement, all feeling, all thinking is possible because of *lung*—there is no movement without *lung*. *Lung* is rooted in an area about four finger widths below the navel (roughly similar to the *tan-tein* energy in Qigong practice). That is its home, so to speak, from which it flows through the channels carrying the sparks of life that convey the vitality that sustains our physical, mental, and emotional condition.

But since we can't see the subtle body or touch it, how do we know it's there?

EMBRACING EMBARRASSMENT

It took me several years to discover an answer to this question, and only then through a rather embarrassing incident that occurred during my first teaching job in North America.

It had been a long flight from Nepal to California, and when I finally arrived, the woman coordinating the retreat looked me up and down. "Rinpoche, you look terrible!" she exclaimed. "Would you like me to arrange for a physical therapist?"

Gratefully, I agreed.

After a couple of days of working out the arrangements, the therapist arrived at the place where I was staying. She was a bit scary-looking, I admit, dressed in black leather studded with bits of metal, but I let that pass. She instructed me to lie down on one of the twin beds in my room and commenced to wave her hands over my body, every once in a while lightly brushing me with a slight, tickling movement. I felt some sort of tingling, but it wasn't the kind of deep-tissue therapy I was hoping for to relieve the knots and kinks in my body. After half an hour she asked me to turn over on my back (which took a couple of moments, because my robes had gotten a little bit tangled), and as she continued to do her hand-waving, I started to feel a little bit grumpy and an inner story started churning.

"She said she would work for an hour," I thought. "Half an hour has passed, and still she hasn't touched me. Well, maybe she's just trying to find out in her own way exactly where my knots are. Then, once she finds them, she'll dig them out."

She did a bit a bit more hand-waving and a slight, tickling sort of touching. Then she grabbed my right hand and slowly brought my arm up and down and around and at that moment I thought, angrily, "What kind of therapy is this? I can move my arm around myself."

Suddenly she shouted at me from the other bed, "Rinpoche, either I'm doing the work or you are!"

I wondered what she was talking about. Then I opened my eyes, and saw that my arm was completely frozen, outstretched, and at a right angle to my body. All that inner grumbling, all that expectation, all those pessimistic feelings had literally frozen my arm. She'd already let go of me, but my arm was still hanging there.

I was so embarrassed. Instantly, I let my arm drop.

She did a little work on the arm; then it was time for her to leave. Afterward she asked me when I would like another session, and I just mumbled something about another few days.

But after she left and I thought about it, I really saw the connection between the subtle body and the physical body. My emotions had completely taken over my physical responses.

It was a revelation to experience firsthand the effects of the subtle body. Although it was at first embarrassing, after a while I began to appreciate the embarrassment and even embrace it—perhaps because I'm a little bit backward. I respect the teachings of past masters, but until I experience something for myself, they don't make a lot of sense to me.

A QUESTION OF BALANCE

Ideally, the subtle body is in balance. The channels are open, the wind is centered in its "home" and blows freely through the channels, and the sparks of life flow easily. We feel a certain sense of lightness, buoyancy, openness, and warmth. Even though we may have a lot planned for the day, or face a long drive or maybe an important meeting, we feel calm and confident. We look forward to whatever the day ahead presents: a state of being that could be called "being happy for no reason."

On the other hand, we can wake up to exactly the same circumstances—the same bed, the same room, the same plans for the day—and feel heavy, angry, depressed, or anxious. We don't want to get out of bed, and when we finally do we hide behind a newspaper or a computer screen. We're "unhappy for no reason"—or at least no reason we can readily identify.

Which is one reason why the subtle body is called "subtle." The interaction of *tsa*, *lung*, and *tigle* are difficult to detect until an imbalance emerges full-blown in some sort of emotional, physical, or mental difficulty or challenge. Patterns that develop on the level of the subtle body often form without our direct conscious awareness and, if left unattended, can grow over the years until they burst onto the scene, so to speak.

THE CAUSES OF IMBALANCE

There are two major routes through which the subtle body can become imbalanced.

One involves the *tsa*, which can become blocked or twisted, usually after some kind of shock or trauma. For example, several years ago I was traveling by airplane between Pokhara—one of the lowland regions in central Nepal—to Muktinath, a remote site high in the Himalayas. It was a very small plane, with only about eighteen seats, most of which were filled by foreign tourists, most of whom were religious pilgrims.

I was traveling to Muktinath to oversee the Buddhist nunnery there. The temples and other buildings had fallen into disrepair, and the nuns' living conditions were appalling. There simply wasn't enough funding or enough skilled workers to maintain them.

The plane was supposed to depart at 8:00 A.M. in order to avoid the high winds that almost always develop later in the day. But in those days airplane travel in Nepal was an uncertain prospect at best, and planes often departed hours later than they were supposed to. Eventually we left the airport, three and half hours after the plane was scheduled to depart and long after the winds had begun to blow.

As we flew between two huge mountains, our tiny plane was buffeted up and down by turbulence for almost half an hour. Many of the passengers were screaming and crying, sure they were going to die. I applied a little method that helped steady me a bit: Instead of focusing on the movement of the plane, I looked out the window and focused on one of the mountains. But I must admit I was infected by the same fear that engrossed the other passengers. That fear—that shock to my nervous system imprinted a kind of twist in my *tsa*. Though we landed safely, I prayed that there might be another way to get back to Pokhara— by car or bus; but the only route in those days was flying. On the return trip, crammed in the same small plane with foreign tourists, I sweated so badly my robes began to get wet. I clutched the armrests tightly, and though doing so made me feel a little better, a part of me knew that no matter how tightly I clutched, it wasn't going to help if the plane really crashed.

When such a scary event occurs, the rational mind becomes a bit senseless and *tsa* get twisted, forming patterns that affect not only our emotional reactions but our physical reactions as well.

The repetition of disturbing experiences throughout life can also cause a kind of twisted pattern to be imprinted on the *tsa*. For example, one woman recently confided that as a child she was urged by the adults in her life to "keep your mouth shut . . . never complain, never explain." Now, whenever she tried to speak about what she was thinking or feeling, her throat closed up and her mouth became dry. She's caught in a marriage with someone who abuses her, but she can't speak about it. Every time she picks up the phone to call an emergency number, her fingers go numb, her voice fails.

The other major type of imbalance occurs when the *lung* becomes agitated. This type of imbalance often evolves along with the development of the various layers of "I." As soon as we enter into the realm of the "solid I" (and by extension, the "solid other"), we become susceptible to hope and fear, attraction and aversion, praise and prejudice.

Because we're cut off from the basic spark of essence love, clarity, and openness that is our nature, we begin seeking fulfillment outside ourselves—through accomplishments, acknowledgments, relationships, acquisitions. But because in almost all cases we're disappointed by what we seek, and because what we find doesn't really fill that empty space, we keep on seeking, keep on trying harder, and that *lung* or energy within us becomes agitated. Consequently we become restless and speedy; our hearts race; we have trouble sleeping.

That restless energy feeds on itself. Without realizing it, we walk faster, talk faster, and eat faster. Or we suffer headaches, backaches, anxiety, or nervousness. Even when we're ready to go to sleep or perhaps take a little nap, we're plagued by an uneasiness—what I've learned to call an internal "speediness"—that simply won't allow us to rest. Our *lung* is asking us to do something, but we don't know what.

For example, a student of mine recently described a situation in which, while physically exhausted by a work project, he was given an opportunity to take a nap in a hammock outside the home of a friend on a soft summer day. He was surrounded by fragrant flowers and the sounds of birds chirping.

"But I couldn't sleep," he explained. "Something kept churning inside, a feeling that I was wasting my time, that I needed to get back to work. There were phone calls and e-mails to answer. I had so much to do."

"That something," I explained to him, "is your *lung*. It's stuck in a pattern. *Lung* is a little blind. A subtle inner restlessness that is not in the mind or the body is not going to let you rest, no matter how tired you are."

This subtle inner restlessness can evolve into a very dangerous situation. If we don't address it, the disturbed *lung* can settle into the heart or other physical systems. We may become feverish, our eyes burning, our skin feeling too tight. We may sweat through nights of interrupted sleep, rolling back and forth to find a comfortable position, while our *lung* keeps throbbing, provoking all sorts of thoughts, feelings, and physical sensations. Sometimes we may settle on a rational explanation for our distress—a deadline, an argument, financial anxieties, or health problems—but even if the apparent issue is identified, the restlessness continues.

When that energy becomes too intense, we can even feel exhaustion, sluggishness, and depression. We feel burned out, listless, unable to perform even the simplest tasks. We find ourselves sleeping more and more throughout the day, though troubled by disturbing dreams.

In addition, once an imbalance occurs, *lung* can become trapped somewhere, usually in areas correlating to our upper bodies—for example, our heads or our chests. A good friend of mine had so much pain in his neck and shoulders that he actually asked his friends to walk on his upper body while he lay on his stomach. But that was only a temporary solution, which had to be repeated every day.

For many of us, imbalances form patterns that seem to have lives of their own. *Tsa* become blocked. *Lung* begins to travel crazily or intensely. *Tigle* get stuck or move around in a holding pattern, like airplanes circling over an airport waiting to land. Over time, these patterns begin to shape our thinking, feeling, and behavior without our ever realizing it.

Because these patterns live, so to speak, in the subtle body, we have to approach them carefully, with the same kind, gentle, alert attention with which we approached our physical bodies. We begin by paying attention to the alarms raised by the subtle body, while recognizing that they represent only one aspect of our experience.

EIGHT

Learning to Ride

One of the analogies Tselwang Rindzin used as we sat together in the fading light on that long-ago afternoon was that the relationship between the mind and the subtle body is like the relationship between a rider and a horse. When the rider is too tense or too pressured, it can make the horse go a little crazy. When the horse is wild, it can make the rider crazy.

I mentioned this analogy recently to a student of mine who loves horses and often goes riding in the woods. He told me that it sounded very similar to the way he learned to handle horses when they become restless.

"Horses react to anything they think might be dangerous by running away mindlessly," he said. "They'll run anyplace. They're panicked and confused. So the rider has to reassure the horse to calm it.

"The best way to handle a disturbed horse," he continued, "is to be kind and clear about what you want and expect. Be sure the horse understands. Go slow. Don't keep pushing when the horse is confused. Once they get it right, then let go. The horse feels good that it did what you wanted correctly. This is how horses learn."

This is also how the subtle body learns: through kind, gentle direction and a willingness to let go when it finds its own balance.

How do we begin?

UNGLUING

On the level of feelings, whatever discomfort, speediness, restlessness, and so on that we experience is typically the result of assuming that horse and rider are identical. So we begin working with the subtle body by simply establishing some sort of distinction between them, an understanding that what we're feeling does not finally or formally define who we are. Our "I"dentities may be influenced by patterns in the subtle body, but we are *not* those patterns. The horse is not the rider; the rider is not the horse.

In many cases, our sense of who and what we are is trapped by patterns established in our subtle bodies. We experience such patterns, more often than not, as troubling emotions. The essential condition—the "glue" that makes this trap especially sticky—is the habit of assuming the "solid I" as absolutely, rather than relatively, real.

For instance, I heard recently from a woman who has been an emergency-room nurse for many years.

"Over time," she wrote, "I've developed a feeling that I have to do something to take away their pain. Reason and experience, of course, tell me that I am not responsible for their pain. Yet after twenty-five years, somehow it has seeped into me that if their pain is appearing in my sphere of awareness, I'm somehow responsible for the outcome—whether it's alleviation of the pain or an increase in pain, confusion, and even death.

"When a patient's pain increases, or if he or she dies," she continued,

"I feel it's my fault. I didn't do enough or I should have done better. In other words, whatever happened to a patient was my responsibility.

"What I've learned through the teachings on the subtle body is a way of establishing a dialogue and bringing a bit of light into that identification—to talk to the places in my subtle body where patterns of responsibility 'live,' so to speak. To realize that they are not 'me'—or not the total 'me.' That they are deposits—or what you sometimes call residue—of memory, which need to be acknowledged, felt, caressed, and released into a greater flow of openhearted caring.

"Sure, you gave a lot of technical explanation about the subtle body, but what struck me most was a little phrase you used to describe dealing with emotions: 'Honey, we have to talk.'

"It reminded me so much of the way my husband and I deal with each other and with our kids. So humane. So simple. It never occurred to me that I could work with my own feelings in the same way as I deal with my family. But it opened my eyes. My husband isn't me. My kids aren't me. In the same way my emotions aren't me. But instead of trying to confront them angrily or resentfully, there was a way to gently start a conversation.

"Honey, we have to talk."

DIALOGUE

How many times have we heard this opening? How rarely, though, have we initiated it as a means of engaging our own experience?

In order to unglue, to brush away the residue that feeds our "I"magination, we need to practice becoming attentive to the tendency to identify with and as our feelings—to recognize that they're only one aspect of experience and not the totality. That's the basic practice of

Mindfulness of Feeling. It's a method through which we reassure our subtle body and alert it to the habit of identifying with and as our emotions.

Try practicing that the next time you feel a strong emotion. Tell yourself that whatever you're experiencing is not the total "I," that what you're feeling is only one piece of your experience—in a kind and reassuring way, not blaming the feeling or the pattern behind it but rather offering it a place in your attention in which to come to rest.

You might begin by talking to your *tsa.*

For example, after that bumpy flight to Muktinath, I began traveling around the world a great deal. The same fear, the same sweatiness, the same urge to clutch the armrests overtook me even though I was now traveling on much larger and more powerful planes and never encountered the kind of turbulence I felt in the mountain passes of Nepal. For three years I tried everything—praying, meditating, staring out the window, reading—but still that imprinted fear would take over.

Finally I realized I could just talk to my *tsa*: that is, recognize, acknowledge the feeling as a feeling, a part of experience, but not necessarily my whole "I." At that point of just recognizing and acknowledging the feeling, I began to speak to it very kindly, in effect saying, "Hello! I understand why you're here. Feel free to stay, but I'd just like to point out, if you care to notice, that the circumstances are completely different. Feel free to hang out if you want, just know that there's no reason for you to stay if you don't want to."

Of course, patterns imprinted on the *tsa* can become much more intense when *lung* is agitated or intense, so we must also learn how to work with *lung*, as well.

The first step in working with *lung* is to understand that when *lung* is agitated or intense, it's not actually the *lung* we're feeling, it's the pressure of the *lung* against the *tsa*, which is experienced sometimes as emotions and sometimes as physical sensation. When we see where it presses or how it presses, that gives us some indication of where the *lung* is most agitated, intense, or stuck. So we begin by closing our eyes and taking a few moments to simply bring attention to where we feel the greatest discomfort or restlessness.

Is your neck sore?

Are your shoulders tense?

Is your heart racing?

Are you sweating a lot?

Does your head feel heavy?

Try, if you can, to refrain from the tendency to be a strict "rider" at this stage. Another horse rider recently wrote, "I often think of all the feelings and thoughts I'm telegraphing to my horse when I'm riding her, and that she's picking up every single clue and responding to every one. I can tell when she gets nervous that she really needs me to stay calm, to guide her, to give her confidence."

Where and how does this capacity to communicate calmness and confidence emerge?

The spark.

As one woman, who suffers from rheumatoid arthritis, described it: "I look into the essence of whatever I'm feeling and recognize that what I'm experiencing is not the total me, not the whole me. Yes, I experience pain, but I also feel love toward my husband, my children, and my grandchildren. That helps. Whatever pain I'm feeling is only one part of a larger experience. Pain is only part of my experience. Love is much greater. I want to be around my husband, my kids, and my grandkids. I enjoy being around them. Of course, they realize that my bones and muscles hurt, and they help in certain household tasks. But they recognize that I'm not going to give up doing my share, and they respect that. And I respect them for recognizing that. Out of this something

148

quite new has developed. I used to be a single-minded, devoted mother, devoted to taking care of everyone. Now everyone participates in some way.

"I want to cry when one of my grandkids asks, 'Can I clear the table, Grandma?' or 'Can I dry the dishes?'

"Such a feeling of companionship, of consideration, was never a part of our household. Now it's become a kind of new normal.

"As this transformation is happening, I find the pain in my body decreasing bit by bit. My bones don't hurt as much.

"Maybe I'm being a little selfish in not letting my family know that I'm not feeling so much pain. But to see them come together like this, to—what can I call it?—finding their own hearts, to making connections with each other, it makes me happy. Like I've accomplished a little something as a mother and a grandmother. Maybe that will just stay within the family, but wouldn't it be nice to think that these children and grandchildren would extend that kindness to other people in the world?

"I'm old. I might never live to see it happen. But I like to think that it's possible."

VASE BREATHING

One of the methods that helped this woman and countless others cope with emotions is a practice that helps us to draw *lung* back to its center, or "home." For this, we use a special breathing technique as a tool, because breath is a physical correlation to the subtle wind energy of the *lung*.

This technique is called *vase breathing*, and it involves breathing even more deeply than the type of deep diaphragmatic breathing often taught in many yoga and other types of classes with which people may be familiar.

The technique itself is rather simple. First, exhale slowly and completely, collapsing the abdominal muscles as close to the spine as possible. As you slowly breathe in, imagine that you're drawing your breath down to an area about four finger widths below your navel, just above your pubic bone. This area is shaped a bit like a vase, which is why the technique is called vase breathing. Of course, you're not really drawing your breath down to that region, but by turning your attention there, you will find yourself inhaling a bit more deeply than usual and will experience a bit more of an expansion in the vase region.

As you continue to draw your breath in and your attention down, your *lung* will gradually begin to travel down there and begin to rest there. Hold your breath down in the vase region just for a few seconds—don't wait until the need to exhale becomes urgent—then slowly breathe out again.

Just breathe slowly this way three or four times, exhaling completely and inhaling down into the vase area. After the third or fourth inhalation, try holding a little bit of your breath—maybe 10 percent—in the vase area at the end of the exhalation, focusing very lightly and gently on maintaining a bit of *lung* in its home place.

Try it now.

Exhale completely and then breathe slowly and gently down to the vase area three or four times, and on the last exhalation, hold a little bit of breath in the vase area. Keep this up for about ten minutes.

How did that feel?

Maybe it was a little uncomfortable. Some people have said that directing their breath in this way is difficult. Others have said that doing so gave them a sense of calmness and centeredness they'd never felt before.

Vase breathing, if practiced ten or even twenty minutes every day, can become a direct means of developing awareness of our feelings and of learning how to work with them even while we're engaged in our daily activities. When our *lung* is centered in its home place, our bodies, our feelings, and our thoughts gradually find a healthy balance. The horse and rider work together in a very loose and easy way, neither trying to seize control or drive the other crazy. In the process, we find that subtle body patterns associated with fear, pain, anxiety, anger, restlessness, and so on gradually loosen up, that there's a little bit of space between the mind and the feelings.

Ultimately the goal is to be able to maintain that small bit of breath in the vase area throughout the day, during all our activities—walking, talking, eating, drinking, driving. For some people, this ability becomes automatic after only a short while of practice. For others, it may require bit more time.

I have to admit that, even after years of practicing, I still find that I sometimes lose my connection to my home base, especially when meeting with people who are very speedy. I'm a bit of a speedy person myself, and meeting other speedy people acts as a kind of subtle body stimulus. I get caught up in their restless and displaced energy and consequently become a bit restless, nervous, and sometimes even anxious. So I take what I call a reminder breath: exhaling completely, breathing down into the vase area, and then exhaling again leaving a little bit of breath in the *lung*'s home.

REORIENTATION

Balancing the subtle body through the various practices discussed above can feel a bit disorienting at first because the patterns of imbalance have become so much a part of who we think we are.

"I actually enjoyed being restless and speedy," one student recently admitted. "I felt I was doing something in my job. I didn't realize at the time what a toll it was taking on my physical body or that I was becoming somewhat snappish with my coworkers. I actually enjoyed bossing them around, and never realized the atmosphere of bitterness and tension I was creating.

"Then, one day, someone I was working with confronted me. 'You're a bitch,' she told me. 'You manufacture crises that don't exist, only to prove your importance and I won't put up with it any longer.'

"Of course, I was shocked—not only because of her outspokenness but because I hadn't recognized how outlandish I'd become, how convinced of my own importance.

"After some consideration, I began to understand that I believed that if I let go of my agitated, intense energy, I wouldn't be able to accomplish anything. I wouldn't be able to express myself. Maybe I wouldn't feel anything at all. Maybe I'd become as motionless or expressionless as stone.

"But after that confrontation—and a couple of similar ones like it—I realized I was wrong. My approach, my focus, had practically turned me into a stone.

"It's hard to change when you've been doing things one way for many years. It's like trying to turn around a battleship. And that's how I'd kind of come to see myself, as a battleship. I'm not saying I've turned into a sailboat. But maybe something a little lighter, easier to turn and change direction.

"I don't know if that's a good analogy, but I'm slowly coming around to the idea that I've been very hard on myself and, because of that, I've been very hard on others. I'm more receptive to other people's opinions now. I don't feel that every decision is a life-or-death choice.

"Actually that first confrontation, shocking as it was, has helped me ease up a little on myself. I don't have to be the most important person in the room, which was something I believed for too many years. I find myself relaxing a little bit more just by listening to other people and by not running them over with my own ideas."

When we begin to practice Mindfulness of Feeling, gently engaging with our subtle bodies, we'll find it easier to accomplish much more than we ever could have believed possible. The key point in working with the subtle body lies in noticing our feelings and learning to welcome them, to accept them, and to relate with them rather than allowing them to take over or trying to control them or push them away.

In simple terms, we learn through working with the subtle body that whatever emotions we experience are not the totality of our being.

Yes, they are a part of our experience—but only a part.

We can work with them, breathe with them, and welcome them into our "home." Ultimately, feelings are only guests. They arise and emerge as a result of various conditions, but they're not permanent residents.

The ultimate goal of the Dharma is to assist us in seeing what's true—and the truth is that though we act out our daily lives in a realm of relative reality that emerges, abides for a while, and dissolves as various causes and conditions temporarily come together, in absolute terms reality is unimaginably free, unimaginably open. At the same time, relative reality and the absolute reality complement each other. We cannot hold ourselves as something, as somebody defined by this or that characteristic or combination of characteristics or attributes. From time to time we need to come home to the simple fact that ultimately we can't be defined by our circumstances and just allow ourselves to rest in that openness.

Approaching our experience in this way is a bit like staying in hotel. We know we don't own the hotel, but at the same time we live in a room there for a few days. We enjoy our stay, but we are respectful guests.

We don't burn the carpet or steal the towels. In the same way, we must respect the relative reality in which we function. We take from it what we need, but we don't really own it. If we approach our experience with that kind of attitude, life starts to be more enjoyable, no matter what our circumstances. We can deal with adversity in our own lives and assist those in need with greater courage and conviction.

NINE

The Inner Speed Limit

I've always enjoyed my trips to college towns like Boulder, Colorado. In the restaurants and cafés where students gather, I can usually see a "juiciness"—a sense of being alive and being in love with being alive—in the young women and men gathered there; an excitement about being able to debate, to share their emotions, to agree to disagree.

But every once in a while I'll see someone who looks old before his or her time, sitting in a corner bent over notes or a book. I've always wondered how this happened. How could the spark of aliveness be dimmed in one so young?

The answer came to me a few years ago when I was on an airplane traveling from New York to California and overheard a conversation between a father and his daughter who were sitting in the row behind me. The daughter looked to be about twelve or thirteen years old and she was crying almost throughout the entire flight because her father was lecturing her about responsibility. From what I overheard, the father kept hammering at her that she wasn't being responsible; that she wasn't spending enough time on her schoolwork; that she was spending too much time on the phone with her friends; that she spent too

much time listening to music; on and on and on. He seemed to be trying to be reasonable with her, but his tone was so cold and insistent.
"You need to be more disciplined in your life," he kept telling her, "or
else how are you going to achieve anything, how are you going to get
anywhere in the world? The world is a competitive place, and if you
don't work hard now, you'll pay for it later."

He continued lecturing her for six hours, all the way from New
York to California. As I listened, I couldn't help but think that while he
may have been trying to teach her about responsibility, he was, on
some level, teaching her fear. And even with the best of intentions, fear
is what we take in alongside our lessons about goals and achievement.
It becomes a part of the pattern imprinted on the subtle body.

Of course, it's difficult to resist this dual lesson, especially when
we're young. But even as adults, many of us find it difficult to discover
a balance between the demands of the intellect and the subtle work-
ings of emotion. In many ways, our social or cultural environment not
only shapes the patterns that define our experience but also reinforces
them.

Day by day, moment by moment, we receive so much information.
So many demands are placed on our attention. Our lives have become
in some ways like modern news programs that have split screens showing a newscaster in one window, someone being interviewed in another,
stock market information in another, maybe another news story playing
in another, and underneath it a crawler with a breaking news story.

As we try to take in all this information, our minds, our subtle bodies, and our physical bodies become somewhat unbalanced. We feel
that if we're not looking at all these things at once that we're missing
something, so we push ourselves. We multitask. We hurry, hurry, hurry
to get whatever it is we're involved in at the moment finished so we can
get on with the next project of the day, and the next, and the next. And

all that hurrying saps a great deal of our mental, emotional, and physical energy—which tends to make us less productive, more volatile emotionally, and more muddled in our thinking.

DRIVING TO WORK

So it becomes important to find a balance between thoughts, feelings, and physical experiences—to discover what I refer to as our "inner speed limit," a comfortable margin of activity that allows us to complete the tasks with which we're faced on a daily basis without receiving a mental, emotional, or physical "speeding ticket."

To use an example from my own life, several years ago I was asked by Adeu Rinpoche to work on a project that involved gathering as many of the teachings of the Drukpa Kagyu lineage as possible. The texts of these teachings had been scattered over many years among different areas of Tibet, as well as in different countries like Nepal, India, and Bhutan. Many of them were only partially complete or had been copied or recopied over the years with errors or ambiguities that had to be sorted out and refitted into their proper contexts. In all there were about 113 volumes, each consisting of some 300 pages that had to be sorted, reformatted, and recombined.

I would drive daily to a decaying office building in Boudhanath, about a forty-five-minute trip south from my home through twisted, sometimes unpaved roads, often crowded with cars, trucks, rickshaws, people—even goats and cows.

During the course of the project, I started feeling a great deal of stress. My "social I" started to take over all my interactions. I wanted to complete this project, not just to preserve the teachings but also so that I would look good in the eyes of one of my teachers. Maybe there was a little bit of "precious I" involved, too, because completing the project involved some sort of personal gratification.

Over time, though, I noticed that I'd started to feel overwhelmed by the task, which was interfering with my duties at a monastery I was in charge of, the oversight and rebuilding efforts of several nunneries in my care in Nepal and Tibet, and spending time with my family. I'd make mistakes, so things had to be recopied, rewritten, and reprinted.

One day, while I was driving to Boudhanath, I noticed how internally "speedy" I was—mentally, emotionally, and physically tense as I rushed to get to the office. By the time I got there, I was already exhausted. So I began talking to myself. "Okay, you're just driving. However long it takes you to get there—forty-five minutes, one hour, two hours—you don't have to let yourself get speedy inside. You can just go along at a normal speed limit and not worry about traffic, cows, or goats. However long it takes, it doesn't matter." I decided to just drive along, without rushing, without the pressure to get there—and arrived at the office at exactly the same time as I usually did, but without the sense of being exhausted or rushed.

That experience of talking myself down was a big buddha moment. I realized that it wasn't the amount of work or the deadlines that sapped me of my vitality; it was a habit of exceeding my internal speed limit. That didn't mean that I had to drive any slower or give up on the deadlines or somehow change my outer environment. I just had to learn to manage the way my subtle body patterns were intensified or exacerbated by the demands and challenges of my life.

I think at some point we all feel such pressure. A man who worked in an accounting firm recently described how each day the head of his office would demand facts and figures that he couldn't immediately produce—mostly because they had to pass through various departments that included marketing expenditures, advertising costs, and actual sales. He began to resent his boss (as many people did). But then his boss developed cancer, and even though she underwent several operations and treatments, she died.

"Did I know she was ill?" he replied, when asked. "Yes. Did I think that her illness came from pressure from people who rated her performance? Maybe. Perhaps there were other factors involved, like a predisposition to cancer that was exacerbated by stress.

"Did I wish she would die? No. I hoped she would retire. I hoped that she would recognize that she was in a difficult position, and maybe force the people above her to recognize that they were making unreasonable demands. She wasn't easy to get along with most of the time, but part of me recognized that she was doing her best to answer to her bosses. And her best, apparently, wasn't good enough. And it killed her.

"I have to confess that for a long while I hated her, but I didn't wish that she would die. She was under so much pressure, she caused a lot of heartache for the people working under her. We were all working beyond our capabilities, faster and faster, and we made mistakes.

"She took those mistakes too personally, and that, I think, was what killed her."

FINDING THE SPEED LIMIT

I've found that if I followed my inner speed limit, the people with whom I was working became calmer and more productive. My directions were clearer, fewer mistakes were made, and the people engaged in the project began to actively enjoy their work. Once I stopped rushing, the people around me stopped rushing, too. It seemed like everyone began to find their own inner speed limit. A kind of collective sigh of relief passed through the office now that "the boss" had become a less demanding guy. I noticed, too, a physical relaxation in the way they worked.

Not everyone has the same inner speed limit, of course. Finding our internal speed limit involves a process of first recognizing our thoughts, feelings, and physical sensations as part of the ongoing process of being alive and then learning to discover a balance among them.

When seeking our own personal speed limit, rather than concentrating on the degree of effort we typically expend in accomplishing certain tasks or the number of tasks we accomplish, a more productive approach might be to consider the manner in which we approach such tasks. Do we consider the opportunities and challenges ahead of us with kindness and warmth, or do we just get through them in a brusque, impersonal way? When we get in our cars and face another driver at an intersection, do we let him or her through first with a little wave of our hand or acknowledge that the driver will let us through first with a wave or a "thumbs-up" gesture? Such small kindnesses can influence the way we deal with ourselves and others, learning to balance our focus on our own busy, multitasking lives, developed over many years, to accommodate, even in small ways, the needs of others, who are themselves trying to accomplish many things at once.

We have the capability to discover our own internal rhythms through mindfulness practices—those already discussed and those yet to be described—and slowly, gently, kindly reconnecting with that spark of openness, clarity, and warmth that is the centerless center of our being. We know we've begun to find a healthy balance when we feel our own restlessness, speediness, or tension begin to lower; when we begin to take a more relaxed attitude toward whatever project we're undertaking. For example, when a student of mine who works for a public relations firm was assigned a project that had to be completed "five minutes before yesterday," he would break out into hives. Gradually he learned that if he took a little bit more time on the project, he not only stopped breaking out but actually produced better work, which resulted in better results for the company he worked for.

"I was also less angry," he said, "less frightened that I would lose my job. I focused on the project, not the timeline, and in doing so—even though I didn't produce something 'five minutes before yesterday'—what I handed in was clearer, cleaner, with fewer mistakes. I also felt a bit prouder of what I handed in.

"In part, too, I noticed that my attitude toward the people I worked with changed. All too often, I totally ignored them. I felt there was little time to interact. I hated the chitchat among them, which I felt was a distraction. Now I can listen to their conversations and even participate—and in doing so, I learned a few new techniques for using the Internet for research and a few new words to express certain ideas.

"But perhaps most important, I've seen a change in their attitude toward me. They don't avoid me when I'm working on a project. They ask if they can help. They offer suggestions. And I listen. I take a moment to thank them for their help.

"There's less tension in the office now, and more of a sense that we're all working together toward a common goal."

LOOPS

It's possible that the habit of exceeding one's internal speed limit can become a self-destructive loop if it continues for too long. On a very subtle level, it can be emotionally and intellectually inhibiting and unproductive. Most of us don't notice these loops until someone points them out to us.

At that point, we're confronted with a choice: We can change our pattern, we can lower our speed limit, or we can carry on as usual.

Some people choose to carry on. They enjoy the anger, tension, and disturbance they create. Some people recognize that the conflict they engender doesn't serve their personal or professional interests, and choose—perhaps reluctantly, perhaps slowly—to amend their approach.

Such a choice can be life-altering. A young woman who was a leader of a charitable organization came to realize that her ambition to become the head of the organization conflicted with the goals of the organization.

"I wanted to be important," she said. "I wanted to be famous. But would that help the organization? No, I realized. After looking at what I wanted and what the people who were being helped by the organization needed, I realized that the people who were in need were more important than I was. I'd set myself on a speed track to take over the organization. I was exhausting myself every day trying to become the head of the group, and I was ignoring the goals of the group."

Exhaustion is one of the ways we recognize that we've exceeded our internal speed limit. We find ourselves unable to rest, to sleep, to even dream. Shutting ourselves off from casual interactions with others is another. We don't feel we have time for watercooler or coffee conversations. We make excuses for not meeting friends for lunch or dinner.

As one student put it, "My social life came to a standstill. I made nice apologies for refusing lunch or dinner invitations, telling people I was caught up in a project. But really, I was speeding.

"Why was I speeding? Because I was terrified. I was afraid that someone at work would speed ahead of me, and in this environment, losing a job is a scary thing. If I lost my job, I could lose my house. Maybe my kids could be taken away to foster homes. These worries kept me up at night, and I probably made decisions that were not in the best interests of the company I worked for. But I had my home to consider, my children, and how to keep food on the table.

"I started reaching out to other people. I accepted lunch and dinner invitations. And when I did, I discovered that I was not alone. A lot of people were scared. We talked, we ate and drank—cheaply. The best thing is that we banded together. We made a decision that our personal lives were as important as our professional lives. That 'getting ahead' didn't just mean getting a promotion—good luck in this job environment— but developing relationships with the people close to us. We made a promise to slow down, to spend more time with each other and with our partners, spouses, and family members."

I found it inspiring how this guy and his friends were able to recognize and acknowledge a common emotional pattern, help each other to work with it, and find a new openness and energy in their lives. I was reminded, too, of how easily thoughts and feelings can become compressed, causing us to behave in ways that are harmful to ourselves and others.

In such cases, a little bit of clarity can go a long way.

HOPE AND A HAMBURGER

A few years ago, I was on my way to a coffee shop in San Francisco near Union Square. I'm quite fond of San Francisco because it's one of the few places I can walk around without the formal robes of a Tibetan Buddhist teacher, just in jeans and a T-shirt. When I teach, of course, I wear my robes, but when I'm not teaching I walk around as an ordinary person, which gives me a chance to engage in less formal conversations that help me to understand the hopes, fears, and concerns of other ordinary people—which better informs my teaching by helping me "take the temperature" of whatever place I'm visiting. When I'm in my robes, even in private meetings with individuals or small groups of students, there's a bit of formality involved; the people I meet with don't open up quite as freely. Their questions tend to focus on philosophical or practical points of Buddhism. When I walk around in ordinary clothing, I find that people are much freer in their conversation, which not only helps me to address their deeper concerns but also assists me in learning bits and pieces of different languages. I've found over the years that people who come to teachings appreciate the fact that I can greet them and say a few words or sentences in their own language. It opens up a direct path to their own hearts and minds.

On this particular morning in San Francisco I left my hotel and headed toward the nearest coffee shop. As I approached the entrance, I heard some yelling and shouting. I looked around and saw a homeless man coming toward me shouting and rolling and banging a garbage bag. I wasn't scared; I just stayed there and looked at him, and he looked at me, and he said to me, "You look like a decent person."

He'd been completely crazy one minute earlier. But when he looked into my eyes, I saw that his eyes were quite clear, and he asked, "Can I have some money?"

I considered that just giving money might be wasted, so I asked him, "Do you want something to eat or drink?"

"Yes," he replied.

"What do you want?" I asked.

"A hamburger," he said.

Unfortunately, hamburgers were only sold in a shop down the street.

"There aren't any hamburgers in this shop. Would you like to come with me and have some other food?"

"Okay," he answered.

As soon as he walked into the coffee shop, he dropped his crazy, noisy behavior. Except for being a little messy, he could have been an ordinary customer.

There was a long line of people ahead of us, as is usual on a Saturday or Sunday morning. So for around five minutes he just stood behind me, not looking anywhere, not doing anything, just standing.

Then I asked, "What do you want to eat?"

Again he said, "A hamburger."

"No," I told him patiently, "there aren't any hamburgers here. Have a sandwich."

We'd reached the head of the line by then, and I could see that the counterperson was becoming impatient with our discussion and a little more than suspicious of my companion. So I quickly chose a sandwich from the available selection and handed it to him. Immediately, he ran out of the shop, and once outside, he started yelling again and banging on walls. Meanwhile, I paid for my purchases and sat at a table drinking my coffee.

Suddenly there was a knock on the window. It was the same homeless guy, saying something I couldn't hear and beckoning to me. I stepped outside to see what he wanted.

"Water," he grumbled.

I realized that while facing the impatience and suspicion of the counterperson that I'd neglected to get him anything to drink. But there was already another long line inside the shop and I couldn't manage enough compassion to stand in it again. So I gave him three dollars and asked, "Can you buy it yourself?"

"Yes," he replied, and went away with his money.

When I returned to my table, I started thinking about how he'd changed so much, so quickly. His ability to think, to organize his speech and behavior seemed to function very well for a little while. But then, on some level—emotional, mental, or perhaps physical—he'd exceeded his internal speed limit and gotten caught in a sort of traffic accident, which repeated itself over and over in a kind of self-destructive loop.

Many of us can get caught up in such loops, but that doesn't mean that we have to get lost in them forever. We have seen how we can begin to untangle certain patterns through working with the subtle body and emotions; but we can bring even greater clarity and openness to our experience through examining our thoughts.

TEN

Minding the Mind

For most of us, thoughts seem very solid, very true. We become attached to them or afraid of them. Either way, we give them power over us. The more solid and true we believe them to be, the more power we give them.

The third foundation of mindfulness—often referred as Mindfulness of Mind or Mindfulness of Thought—involves the practice of noticing the names and labels we attach to our experiences. How often do we tell ourselves, "I'm fat," "I'm ugly," "I'm tired," "I'm a loser," "This person I work with is a total jerk"?

When I was going through some difficult years at Tashi Jong, I labeled myself as "sick." Doctors—well-intentioned—confirmed that diagnosis, though they couldn't agree on a cause of my "sickness." Yes, I had physical symptoms due to stress and was prescribed various remedies. None of them worked, until I had a good long talk with Tselwang Rindzin, who helped me understand that my "sickness" lay in an imbalance of the subtle body.

His advice and instruction brought me back from a desperately confused emotional state. I have to admit that afterward I "borrowed" some other books from the library and, from them, learned that we tend to label our feelings and opinions, and in applying these labels, we tend to fixate on our situations, making them more solid than they might otherwise be.

For example, a woman who'd attended a series of teachings confessed in a private talk that while she had accomplished many things in her life, she felt a deep longing for a lasting relationship. This longing was so intense that she couldn't even look at it in meditation.

When I asked what kind of thoughts she had when she'd experienced this longing for a relationship, she sat quietly for a few moments, and then replied, "I'm unlovable."

After another pause she added, in a whisper, "And maybe I have the idea that other people will think I'm a failure because I've never had a long-term relationship."

Continuing this line of questioning uncovered an assortment of different thoughts and memories, like her mother and father telling her during early childhood that she was clumsy, her nose was too big, her eyebrows were so thick that they met in one line and made her look cross-eyed. "You'll never attract a boy," they said, "and that's your main purpose in life. We'll try to arrange a good marriage for you with someone who won't beat you too much. But that's the best you can hope for, because one look at you and no matchmaker can hope to sell you on your looks."

Secretly, she wanted to be a teacher or a doctor. "But who would want to marry such a woman?" she asked—more of a statement than a question.

Certain developments in the country where she lived have made it possible for her to realize some of her dreams. She became a teacher. "But there aren't many men who want to become involved with women as ugly and clumsy as me."

There was, in fact, an entire "I-story" beneath her longing for a relationship. And when this story was broken down into its various parts, the heaviness of her longing began to lift. Not immediately, of course, but in those moments, it became lighter to bear.

She wasn't ugly, as far as I could see; she wasn't clumsy. She was actually quite intelligent, and though she might not have been pretty according to the standards of her society, her intelligence, her poise, and her ability to talk about her dilemma so clearly gave her a unique attractiveness. She was, in many ways, like the wrestler who'd lost his jewel in his forehead. There was a beauty in her, a warmth, an openness that was obvious to almost everyone except herself.

As she spoke, she was engaging in a type of meditation, reaching into her mind to see what it showed her. Without effort, she began, spontaneously, to apply method and wisdom to her loneliness. This is a crucial point. As she considered each aspect of her predicament, she was meditating, acknowledging on a direct level the thoughts and feelings that had shadowed her for much of her life. As she acknowledged them, some of the judgment she'd held about these thoughts and feelings began to lift, and she was able to break them down into smaller and smaller pieces.

Over the course of our conversation, she experienced, at least momentarily, a shift in perspective. She wasn't someone trapped within the mirror of her loneliness and longing. She *was* the mirror.

Toward the end of the conversation, she took a deep breath.

"I just had a thought," she said. "Maybe my mother felt the same way. Maybe she felt ugly and unlovable. I don't remember ever seeing her happy or smiling. I don't remember seeing my parents laugh together, or embrace, or kiss. And those other girls I grew up with, the pretty ones, the ones who got married . . ."

Her voice trailed off for a moment.

"Were their lives all that terrific?" she asked.

She closed her eyes for a moment, considering.

"Are they happy now? Do they feel alone?"

It was extraordinary to watch this process unfold. Admitting her secret pain allowed her awareness to expand in a manner that enabled her to simply look at it with less judgment than she had while keeping it hidden. In turn, that awareness helped her to break through the label she'd been given, and which she'd adopted, and to break it into smaller pieces, so it didn't seem so fixed. At least in those few moments, her "I-story" began to dissolve.

"Maybe I'm not unlovable," she said. "Maybe I'm not ugly. Maybe I just believed that because I'd heard such things for so long."

Her smile, which lasted only for an instant, was brilliant. If only for a moment, she'd broken through a block that had weighed on her for years. It was great to see her transform, even for a moment, a belief that she was ugly and unlovable and begin to experience a connection to others that transcended desire, jealousy, and fear. In that moment, she was able to shift her perspective, and for a moment she'd reconnected with her spark, she'd touched openness, clarity, and essence love.

This process is the basis of the practice of Mindfulness of Thought, through which we begin to turn our attention to our tendency to bestow hard labels on our experiences. While physical sensations and emotions tend to be quite powerful and can provide vivid objects of focus and alertness, thoughts tend to be a bit more elusive.

CRAWLERS

When we first turn our attention to our thoughts, they can seem like a rushing torrent of judgments, memories, and ideas—which are often intimately hooked to our subtle body patterns. Through working with the subtle body, we begin to create a little space between this immediate, simultaneous connection between our subtle body patterns and the thoughts, or "I"dentifications, that emerge with them.

The speed with which thoughts appear and disappear across the screens of our minds are like out-of-control "breaking news update crawlers" that appear across television screens. We can hardly read one before another takes its place—and another and another. Our awareness is overwhelmed by fleeting impressions, half-grasped notions, bits of sentences, ideas that have only begun to form before they disappear. Typically, we find ourselves trapped in a cycle of trying to keep up with "the news."

In working with many students around the world, I've observed that the "crawler effect" is often the first one most people encounter when they begin to practice Mindfulness of Thought. There are actually several common reactions to this experience.

Many of us are tempted to try to stop the crawlers in the hope of achieving some sort of calmness, openness, and peace. Unfortunately this attempt doesn't help much because it creates a sense of mental and emotional tightness that ultimately manifests as a physical tension, especially in the upper body. Our eyes may roll upward, while our neck and shoulders may become quite stiff.

Sometimes we recognize we've been carried away by the crawlers and try to force ourselves back to simply observing our thoughts. We try to stall the crawlers, so to speak, in an attempt to focus on one thought at a time.

There are a couple of ways through which we can work with such reactions.

If your regret over letting yourself be carried away by them is really strong, then just look at the thoughts of regret. Another method is to shift your attention from thoughts to physical or emotional sensations.

Perhaps your head is a little bit warm, your heart is beating a little faster, or your neck or shoulders are a little stiff. Just rest your awareness on these or other experiences. You might also try simply resting with bare attention on the rush of crawlers itself, just noticing how fast your thoughts come and go. The important point is that, at this stage in the practice, you're becoming familiar with the activity of ordinary awareness, the activity of the mind. Just notice all this activity without judgment.

Of course, in some cases we may experience the opposite effect, in which a crawler becomes stuck, endlessly recycling an old news story that is often based on some sort of subtle or emotional body holding pattern: "So-and-so said something really cruel to me, and I can't forgive him or her." "Oh no, I've got a deadline coming, I'll never be able to complete this project in time!" "I've been out of work for months now. How am I going to feed my family, pay my bills, keep my home?"

But through the practice of being mindful of our thoughts—just lightly being alert to them—we can begin to see that even the ones upon which we fixate are interrupted by other thoughts: "I'm hungry." "I'm lonely." "It's too hot in here." "It's too cold in here." "Oh, I wish this guy would stop droning on and on about mindfulness. Can't he talk about something that will really make a difference in my life?"

As we gradually turn attention to our thoughts, rather than being irritated, disturbed, or carried away by them, we begin to be amazed by their coming and going. We begin to appreciate the entire process of thinking in and of itself—that we're endowed with a capacity that can generate so much mental activity.

In essence, Mindfulness of Thought offers us an opportunity to see how our habitual tendencies to believe our thoughts as solid and true shape our understanding of ourselves and the world around us. "Just as producing waves is a natural function of oceans, lakes, and rivers," as one of my teachers once told me, "thinking is an expression of the mind's capacity to generate judgments, memories, daydreams, and ideas."

Like taking time to become aware of and alert to our physical sensations or feelings, Mindfulness of Thought doesn't involve analysis. We simply notice "Oh, here's a thought. Whoops, there it goes. Here's another thought. There it goes."

Because thoughts can be quite elusive, however, it's best, when we first start out, to practice in an environment that is relatively free of distractions. Most people find it easier, as well, to assume a stable physical position, assuming either the seven-point posture or the three-point posture described earlier.

Next take a few moments to calm your body, perhaps using the technique of noticing your breath.

Then notice the thoughts passing through your mind for maybe two minutes at most.

"I hate this."

"Oh, damn, I forgot to do . . ."

"That guy was such a jerk."

"Why did I send that e-mail?"

"I can't pay my bills."

"I'm sick."

"I'm so old."

"I hate myself."

Whatever passes through your awareness, just notice it. Let it come; let it go. Let it sit there if it sits there.

Then let go of the process. Breathe. Move your body, get on with the tasks ahead of you.

And congratulate yourself. You've just witnessed your mind in action.

TIME AND DISTANCE

As we begin to cultivate a more alert and attentive attitude toward all the thoughts that speed through our minds, the rush begins to calm down a bit. The crawlers get smaller and proceed across our mental screens at a less frantic pace. We become less inclined to identify with our thoughts and begin to develop a sense of "Okay, this is just what is occurring right now." The thoughts that reinforce the stories we tell ourselves become somewhat less noisy or intense, and we begin to "unglue" on a level even deeper than the efforts involved in working with feelings or physical sensations.

More important, as we become mindful of our thoughts, we begin to notice a little distance opening up between our thoughts and the mind that is aware of those thoughts. In modern terms we could compare the practice of Mindfulness of Thought to watching TV or a movie. On the screen, lots of activity may be going on, but we're not actually *in* the movie or the TV show. There's a lot of space between ourselves and whatever we're watching. As we practice observing our thoughts, we can actually experience that same space between our awareness and our thoughts. We're not really creating this space; it was always there. We're merely allowing ourselves to notice it.

After a little bit of practice, we'll find that the rush of thoughts naturally begins to slow, and it becomes possible to distinguish individual thoughts more clearly.

Still, we might not be able to observe each thought as it passes but only catch a fleeting glimpse of it—rather like the experience of having just missed a train or a tram. That's okay, too. That sensation of having just missed observing a thought is a sign of progress, an indication that the mind is sharpening itself to catch traces of movement.

As we keep practicing, we find that we're able to become aware of each thought more clearly as it occurs.

More important, as we become mindful of our thoughts, we gradually become aware of little gaps appearing and disappearing between each thought. In other words, as we're looking at our thoughts, we're also becoming aware of the moments where there are no thoughts. These gaps open out into thought-free moments, experiences of alert awareness and readiness to accept whatever arises or does not arise. Our minds become like doormen at fine hotels, who stand at attention at their posts, letting guests enter and exit but not following them through the hotel.

Through this practice, we begin to connect more directly to the spark that illuminates our being and to move closer to experiencing the vast, open potential that is the basis not only of our own nature but of reality itself.

We also prepare for the next mindfulness practice.

ELEVEN

Inner Space

As mentioned earlier, the Fourth Foundation of Mindfulness, known as Mindfulness of Dharma, can be interpreted in many ways. For me, this particular practice involves resting our awareness in what my father and several of my other teachers called "space."

What does that mean?

Some of you may have already enjoyed a small taste of space in practicing Mindfulness of Body, Feeling, and Thought—or at least have understood the possibility that such practices can help to loosen the knots of "I"dentification that keep us so closely bound to our patterns. In particular, the practice of Mindfulness of Thought can lead us to experience gaps between thoughts in which we're totally alive, alert, and attentive, yet unburdened by the stories we tell ourselves about ourselves, others, and the world around us.

Mindfulness of Dharma practice takes us even further, allowing us to experience a profound sense of openness and clarity that is kindly, warmly welcoming.

It can also be something of a shock.

PREPARATION

After almost a year and a half at Tashi Jong, I heard a rumor that Khamtrul Rinpoche was going to travel to Nepal. I wanted very much to go back to see my father and others in my family, but I didn't know if Khamtrul Rinpoche had made any decisions about who would accompany him. So one afternoon I approached him while he was working on the roof of the main monastery building. I wanted to ask, "Can you take me to Nepal with you?," but I just couldn't figure out how to say it.

I spent hours near him as he worked, but every time I tried to ask, the words stuck in my throat; and the longer I waited, the more anxious I felt and the harder it became for me to even form a coherent thought, much less express it in words. I was caught up in so many layers of "I." On a "solid I" and "precious I" level, I was homesick; I missed the comfort my father and my family offered me. On a "social I" level, I was scared to let Khamtrul Rinpoche know that. I didn't want him to think I was ungrateful for his kindness or unhappy at Tashi Jong.

I'd imagined that if Khamtrul Rinpoche asked why I wanted to go to Nepal, I'd have to come up with a reason—and feeling homesick just didn't seem appropriate. Finally I came up with a solution, which was a bit of a half-truth. Instead of saying I wanted to go to Nepal so I could see my father, I fell back on an excuse that was actually legitimate. In those days, in order to come to India from Nepal, one needed an official letter of permission from the Nepali foreign minister stamped with an official seal. The letter of permission I'd already received, however, granted me only a two-year stay. The time was approaching when the letter had to be renewed. I thought this was a very convenient justification: "I have to go with you to Nepal, or I won't be able to stay in India." I felt terribly stupid about using this excuse; it seemed such an obvious ploy.

But even as I came up with a reason that sounded plausible, I simply blurted out, "I want to go with you to Nepal."

I suspect he probably knew about my internal struggles, though. It doesn't require any special powers to see that an adolescent boy has something on his mind and is embarrassed to talk about it. Khamtrul Rinpoche was very relaxed, though, puttering around with a small smile playing across his mouth. It was such a testament to his kindness that he waited, with a wisp of humor, for me to work out what I had to say.

Nowadays, when my own students demonstrate the same sort of shyness in trying to express themselves, when they want to ask something very personal and perhaps embarrassing, I remember this great teacher's patience and generosity. He didn't ask what I wanted or put words in my mouth. He just waited for me to resolve the conflict in my own way, in my own time, according to my own personality. He let me *be*, just as I was. And in doing so, without any words at all, he communicated that who I was and how I was at that moment were perfectly okay.

That is the mark of a great teacher. The space in Khamtrul Rinpoche's heart was so wide, so open, it included more than enough room to accommodate the needs of an anxious, sweaty fourteen-year-old boy, hovering around, apparently trying to swallow a mouthful of sand rather than admit his own fears and insecurities. For the lucky students who accepted this open warmth, the opportunity of learning from Khamtrul Rinpoche proved to be an immense opportunity.

To my surprise, Khamtrul Rinpoche didn't ask why I wanted to return to Nepal. He didn't say "Yes" or "No." He just said, "Okay." Maybe at that time he hadn't yet made a decision about how many people would accompany him or whom he would choose. The important thing, to my young ears, was that he'd heard my request and had let me know that there was nothing wrong with making it.

In spite of my fears, though, it wasn't all that dramatic a conversation. I'd gone through so much anxiety, all that thinking, for nothing—a great lesson Khamtrul Rinpoche taught, just by being the way he was. There's no need to complicate our lives by twisting and turning to come up with a socially acceptable justification for simple needs and desires. Just say them straight out. What's the worst that can happen? Someone will say "No." Maybe someone will ask "Why do you want this?" or "Why do you need this?" and you will have to justify your request.

In the end, for whatever reasons of his own, Khamtrul Rinpoche chose to take all the young *tulkus* with him on the trip to Nepal. I rode in the same car with him, sitting in front with the driver and another young *tulku*, while Rinpoche sat in back with an older *tulku*, all the way from India to Kathmandu, a journey of fifteen days. A truck carrying some forty monks accompanied us. During the entire journey, Khamtrul Rinpoche was nearly silent—just being—which was a lesson in itself. When we crossed the border and armed officials checked our passports, his peaceful, kind expression never changed. Nothing during our fifteen-day trip upset him.

I accompanied him on his journey to some of the sacred Buddhist sites in Nepal. After two weeks of traveling, I asked him—shyly, because he was still my teacher—if it would be okay to visit my father for a while.

I don't know what I expected, but it was certainly not the broad smile he offered as he said, "That's very good! Please offer my greetings to Tulku Urgyen Rinpoche." He gave me some money to pay for my trip to Nagi Gompa, and a *khata*—a ceremonial scarf symbolizing goodwill and blessings—to present to my father on his behalf.

And so I went, with his gifts and his blessings.

Little did I know what I was in for.

FIRST GLIMPSE

I was able to spend only a few weeks with my father at his hermitage in Nagi Gompa. Near the end of my stay, though, he gave me a lesson in experiencing space.

I'll never forget that first lesson. I was sitting in my father's private room, a small, wood-paneled space with a bed, an altar, and enough room for maybe five or six people to sit. Half of the room was taken up by windows, through which the setting sun shone in golden-red light

He said, "Look at the area around you, with all your senses open, seeing all the objects, feeling all the sensations. Don't block anything. Can you sense that openness, that simple awareness of the things you see, and hear, and feel?"

I nodded.

With the sun setting through windows overlooking a broad valley, the sheer physical warmth of my father's body, his sweet but penetrating gaze, the feeling of the hard wood floor beneath me, it would have been hard *not* to be aware of the multitude of phenomena. And his gentle advice to experience this awareness openly without judgment was a powerful influence. There was something almost magical about the way he could communicate without words or gesture the possibility of appreciating without judgment all the things I saw, heard, and felt.

Then he said, "Now slowly turn that same awareness to the mind that perceives these things openly. Instead of looking at *outer* space, look at *inner* space."

He demonstrated with his hands: turning his palms outward to demonstrate the way we ordinarily perceive by looking outward, and then turning his palms inward to indicate the mind that perceives. Then he let his hands drop into his lap, to demonstrate just letting the whole effort of looking drop—to allow whatever happened happen (or not).

In that moment—due largely to the certainty and understanding he'd cultivated over years of practice—I caught a glimpse of inner space, which is wide open and clear, completely beyond concepts or judgments, in which or through which the entire realm of phenomena appear and disappear. For a brief second or so, I had a direct experience of what in the Buddhist tradition is known as the essence of mind, or the nature of mind: a luminous, limitless awareness that is not chopped up into subject and object, self and other, perceiver and perceived. All distinctions between "the looker" and what was being "looked at" fell away, and for an instant I experienced a complete lack of separation between everything I felt, saw, smelled, and so on, and the awareness that saw, smelled, felt. At that moment, even the effort involved in being mindful *of* something dissolved, and mindfulness became effortless; the clarity, openness, and warmth simply *was*.

It was, as some classic Buddhist texts describe, like waking up in the middle of a dream while still dreaming. I suddenly, unquestionably knew that what I was experiencing was occurring within my own awareness—but it was an experience free from mental, emotional, or physical labels. I had a sensation of immeasurable freedom and possibility, inseparable from the potential to be aware of anything that emerged from that pregnant possibility. It wasn't necessarily an extraordinary, mystical experience, but rather more like a deep sense of relaxation, like settling into a comfortable chair at the end of a long day.

This recognition of the inseparability of awareness from its experience—the awakening in the midst of a dream—was the Buddha's gift to mankind and my father's gift to me.

REACTION

I didn't have enough time at Nagi Gompa to learn from my father all the various means and methods of stabilizing this experience of pure, clear, open awareness.

After returning to Tashi Jong, I started "borrowing" books about meditation from the monastery library, which were not part of the *tulku* curriculum at that point. The main focus in those early years was on reading, writing, memorizing ritual texts, and the various elements associated with performing and participating in rituals.

But after I returned to Tashi Jong, having received that glimpse of the nature of mind, the boisterous, independent spirit I'd known as a child—suppressed for a couple of years while I tried to be a very good *tulku*—began to reassert itself. While I applied myself to the *tulku* curriculum, I secretly began studying some of the classic texts about meditation. Looking back at that time, I can see the value of the slow, gradual training system employed at Tashi Jong and at many other monasteries in Tibet, India, Nepal, Europe, and the Americas—because the lessons presented in those books confused me utterly.

While the early training at Tashi Jong focused exclusively on theory and external conduct, the meditation texts I borrowed from the monastery library dramatized in great detail the positive and negative aspects of what we might call "internal conduct": thoughts and emotions that were labeled "good" or "bad," or in modern terms "negative" or "positive," "constructive" or "destructive." Anger, for example, was the path to hellish realms, where you would spend eons roasting in cauldrons filled with molten lead. Desire could take you to an experience known as the hungry ghost realm, populated by beings with tiny mouths and giant stomachs, who could never be satisfied. Sexual attraction—an especially potent issue for someone who was experiencing the rage of adolescent hormones—was completely off-limits for monks and nuns.

To say that I became confused would be an understatement.

TROUBLE

During my first two years at Tashi Jong, I'd tried very hard to modulate my behavior. Now that I'd been given a glimpse of the nature of my mind, what I saw there horrified me. Thoughts and emotions that weren't particularly "good" or "constructive" kept occurring. I was angry, anxious, competitive, judgmental, and lustful. I came to believe that I was a bad person because I was having thoughts and feelings that classic texts had labeled "bad." A severe and secret judge, almost like a god, took over, watching me, monitoring my thoughts and feelings.

I was so ashamed of my thoughts and feelings that I never shared them with any of my teachers, in large part because they were constantly lecturing about how a *tulku* should be a model of chastity, kindness, charity, and compassion.

"How," I wondered, "could a *tulku* have so many bad thoughts? *Tulkus* are not supposed to have these problems."

My teachers never talked about this dilemma; they never addressed the idea that you could be a *tulku* and still have wild, unpredictable thoughts and feelings.

The conflict between being a good *tulku* and a bad *tulku* became so intense that I could hardly sleep at night. My mind was always churning. "You should be this, you should be that. You should think this, you should think that." I began to hallucinate. Trees, the wind, and even pictures in the monastery temple started speaking to me about my problems. Eventually my body began to deteriorate. I began to sweat profusely. I developed pains in my neck, canker sores, scabs on my head, an acidic churning in my stomach. When I went to see a doctor he said, "You're stressed. Take some vitamin B. That should help."

But the problem wasn't with my physical body. It was with my emotional body and my mind. I was engaged in a kind of epic battle between an external ideal and an internal swarm of thoughts and feelings. Over the next several years I was, as some psychologists might say, fragmenting: falling apart, while still trying to hold myself together.

Sometimes I'd see people laughing, and I'd wonder: "How come they can laugh? How could they be so happy?" I felt as though I was wearing a lamb chop over my head—a thick, raw, meaty shell that kept me from connecting with other people—and constantly fretting about wanting to be good and thinking I was bad.

Although this condition worsened for several years, I consider myself lucky. For many people, such terrible struggles can go on for decades. One student recently confided that she had always considered herself a "replacement child" for an older sibling who had died young. Whether her parents considered her as such cannot be known, but the shrine erected to her deceased sibling in the living room of her parents' home and the pictures of the child in her parents' bedroom convinced her that she wasn't really loved or appreciated for or as herself. With that seemingly unmovable cloud hanging over her experience, she spent more than thirty years trying to prove that she was lovable, admirable, smart, and worthy in her own right—constantly seeking approval from lovers and different groups of friends and coworkers.

Finally all the effort exhausted her. She'd lost her last job, and afterward stayed in bed or shuffled around her apartment for more than six months "like a zombie," as she described it.

"My hair was matted, my teeth were decaying, my apartment was a mess. *I* was a mess."

She laughed.

"That's when I figured I had to take all this Buddhist stuff seriously. I had to start practicing—for real this time. Not to gain some sort of advantage for myself but to really open up to the possibility that I wasn't just a replacement. I was something else. What that was, I didn't know. But I was willing to *not know* for a while and see what happened."

Not knowing, as it turns out, is one of the best possible outcomes when the patterns through which we've identified ourselves begin to crumble—as they inevitably will.

PERFECTLY GREAT

When I was eighteen, I was granted another trip to Nepal. During this second, longer visit with my father, I received deeper teachings about space from the long teaching lineage of *dzogchen*, a Tibetan term that is often translated as "the Great Perfection."

Dzogchen is made up of two words: *dzog*, a contraction of the noun *dzogpa*, which does, on a primary level, mean "perfect" or "perfection," and *chen*, which means "great" or "vast."

But on a subtler level, the word *dzogpa* means "everything is included, nothing is left out." To understand this, imagine sitting in a room looking out through a small window. You see only part of the landscape (or if you're in a city, maybe you only see some parts of the buildings around you—or maybe just the brick wall of the building next door). Then imagine going outside, onto the street. You can see so much more! And if you were to take the time and effort to travel to a more open space, like a park, how much more could you see? And then, if you traveled to an even larger arena—for example, a mountaintop, or the

Grand Canyon, or the top of the Empire State Building, the panorama offered would be even vaster.

In a way, that movement into wider and more open spaces reflects the *chen*, the "great" or "vast" aspect of *dzogchen*. On a more personal level, *chen* may also reflect the sense of exhilaration one feels after walking out of a tiny room with a tiny window and seeing for the first time a much broader scene, a sense that "This is amazing!"

During the two months I stayed with my father on this second visit to Nepal, I received a great many lessons on being able to take in the entire panorama of thoughts, feelings, and sensations that are constantly appearing and vanishing. One of the most memorable teachings came after I'd confessed to him that I had been very confused about the jumble of thoughts and feelings bubbling through my mind, and how I felt like a "bad" *tulku* because I was having "bad" thoughts and feelings.

We were sitting alone together in his small room during the daytime. Through his window I could see clouds forming, floating, and dissolving into different shapes in the sky.

"Look at the clouds," he said. "Are they good or bad?"

I shook my head and tried my best to answer. "Well, they may be good for some people, because it gives them shelter from the sun. But maybe some people might think they're bad, because it might mean rain, which will make them uncomfortable, and maybe pour down too much water on the crops they are growing."

"Exactly," he replied, smiling.

I waited.

"Good, bad, happy, sad—these are relatively true qualities, depending on people's circumstances," he said. "But they aren't absolutely, intrinsically true qualities. On an absolute level they're just labels for experience, which the mind creates and which we cling to as part of ourselves and our experiences. They aren't good or bad in themselves. They're like those clouds floating through space.

"The problem," he continued, "is our tendency to believe wholeheartedly in those labels, which is like trying to hold clouds in space or wishing they would go away. We want to change or hold on to the conditions or circumstances, but that only makes the problem worse because we see these conditions as permanent and intrinsically real, rather than as temporary manifestations of causes and conditions."

As I listened to him, I glanced out the window and saw that indeed the clouds were moving, changing shape, some of them dissipating altogether.

He noticed my glance and murmured, "Yes, look how they're changing. But the *space* beyond them hasn't changed at all. That space is like your essential nature. It doesn't change. It doesn't have a beginning or an end. Just as clouds pass through the sky, sometimes covering it completely, space is always there, in our hearts, in our minds, in all of our experience."

He smiled encouragingly.

"We're just not used to seeing things that way. We see the clouds but not the sky beyond them. We notice our thoughts, we feel our feelings, but we don't see the space that makes it possible to notice such things. We don't see that whatever conditions come together to create such things are only possible because space is open enough to allow them to arise, or that the only reason that they can arise or fade away is that their very nature is space itself."

I pondered this and other lessons for some time. It all seemed like so much abstract philosophy to me.

Then one day, toward the end of my time at Nagi Gompa, I tried an experiment. I went out to the edge of a mountain cliff and sat there, looking at the sky, watching the clouds go by and comparing them to my thoughts. I watched the clouds come and go. I watched my thoughts and feelings come and go. Gradually I began to feel a lightness in my body. The judgments I'd made about myself, my thoughts, my feelings and sensations began to lift. I began to feel very light, even playful: the way I'd felt when I was a child before all this *tulku* stuff invaded my life. I began to feel a spark reigniting in my body as well as my mind. I stopped feeling bad about myself, my thoughts, and my feelings. I began to feel a sense of freedom that I'd longed for since I'd begun my training as a *tulku*.

Maybe, I thought, the different parts of my experience—the high-spiritedness I'd known as a child, the *tulku* training at Tashi Jong, and my father's teachings—could come together in some way. There might be a means of bringing all these different aspects of experience together and becoming a different sort of *tulku*, a bit less formal, a bit more open to listening and responding to the people I would someday be asked to teach.

But again, it was only a glimpse: deeper, perhaps, than what I'd had during my first visit with my father. It would take many years before this glimpse took root and became the abiding principle by which I live my life today.

Of course, the first major development upon my return to Tashi Jong involved talking to Tselwang Rindzin and others among my tutors about the pain and illness I was experiencing. For a long time I'd resisted because they were outwardly quite strict; but I began to consider their outward formidability as a type of cloud that only hid a clear sky, a luminous openness of heart and mind. And that turned out to be the case, as they all encouraged me to find a balance between my mind and my heart, which ultimately led to relinquishing my monastic vows: a difficult decision, but one that I'd come to see didn't really change the essence of my being—the emptiness, the clarity, the love.

THE PRACTICE

The essence of the practice of the Fourth Foundation of Mindfulness is to look beyond the clouds—beyond the judgments of right or wrong, good or bad—and attempt to bring attention to the open space in which judgment, desire, anger, fear, and hope arise as transitory experiences. That open space is where your true nature is revealed—open, loving, and understanding of the difficulties that people undergo in their day-to-day lives.

Traditionally, in order to practice Mindfulness of Dharma, we need to observe what are often translated as "Three Immovabilities": Immovability of Body, Immovability of Sensation, and Immovability of Mind. Practically speaking, these scary-sounding terms are quite simple.

Immovability of Body, for example, means finding a stable physical position, using either the seven-point posture or the three-point posture. Maintaining some kind of anchor to the ground is important in order to maintain a connection to the physical aspect of your being. Keeping your spine as straight as possible keeps the *tsa*, or channels, open, allowing the *lung* to pass freely, carrying with them the *tigle*, the sparks of energy that maintain your life force. All of your physical senses are open to whatever is occurring.

Immovability of Sensation refers to the Mindfulness of Body and Mindfulness of Feeling practices through which we allow ourselves to simply notice the sensations that pass through the physical body and the subtle body. Immovability of Mind, meanwhile, involves just allowing ourselves to be attentive and alert to the thoughts that pass through our awareness.

So take a moment to settle your body . . .

Take a moment to rest in your feelings . . .

Take a moment to rest in your mind . . .

Now allow yourself to simply be aware of what you're aware of. Maybe it's a sound, a smell, a thought, a sensation.

Then turn your attention inward—the way my father had turned his hands—and become aware of what is *aware* of that sound, smell, thought, sensation.

Allow yourself to become aware of and alert to the momentary gaps between physical sensations, feelings, and thoughts, and turn your attention to the space between these clouds of experience. In so doing you may catch a glimpse of the fact that there's no separation, no distinction between the experiences and what is being experienced.

Rest in that glimpse. It might not last for long, maybe a few seconds or so, before the habit of separation arises again. Don't worry. That happens to all of us in the beginning. Just repeat the exercise—becoming aware of whatever you're aware of and then turning your attention inward.

Continue this for a minute or so and then just rest, the way you would after a long day of work.

If you feel up to it again, you can try looking at the gaps for another minute or so.

Then rest. Let go. Take a break.

How was that?

Did you experience any gaps?

Did you see the space in between and around the clouds?

Don't worry if you didn't. I'm still working on it. Perhaps someday I'll be able to achieve the same abilities that my teachers achieved. Until then, I'm just a student, just like you.

ANOTHER METHOD

There is another method of Mindfulness of Dharma practice, which I learned from Nyoshul Khen Rinpoche, one of the great masters of *dzogchen*, who narrowly escaped from Tibet to India in the late 1950s. At first, his life in India was very difficult, and he was compelled to beg in the streets. Gradually, though, as word of his presence spread, he began to teach, drawing large crowds. *Tulkus* who had escaped to India requested teachings from him, and he was invited by several distinguished meditation masters to serve as *khenpo*, or abbot, of the monasteries they'd established in India. Eventually he was invited to share his wisdom in monasteries and retreat centers across Europe, Asia, and the United States.

I had the privilege of meeting him and receiving teachings from him on several occasions. Among the many wonderful things I learned from him was a very simple method of practicing Mindfulness of Dharma, which I share with you now.

Simply breathe in as you raise your arms.

Then exhale sharply as you drop your arms.

Does that sound too easy?

Perhaps.

But in that moment of dropping, you can actually experience a sense of wide-openness, a gap in which there is no separation between experience and experiencer, no solidity, no judgment. Rest in that gap for as long—or as briefly—as it lasts. Don't try to extend it or hang onto it. Simply let it occur, and let it go; then you can try the exercise again.

NO FAILURE

Many people feel some sort of disappointment over not being able to maintain the experience of space. This is especially true for beginners, but even long-term practitioners find that the gap they experience after a few seconds of resting in space becomes crowded with thoughts, feelings, and physical sensations.

But we have to remember that the entire process of building up patterns and "I"dentities has taken a long time and can't be undone in one session, one hundred sessions, or even one thousand. Think of your practice as an exercise program you may start at a gym (except that you don't have to pay any membership fees—as a sentient being, you're already a member). At first you may last a few minutes on a treadmill or stationary bicycle. If you're engaged in weight training you can lift only a few pounds for a few repetitions before your muscles tire. But if you keep at it, gradually you'll find that you can last longer on the treadmill or the bike, or lift heavier weights and perform more repetitions.

Similarly, practicing Mindfulness of Dharma is a gradual process. At first, you might be able to remain alert and attentive for only a few seconds at a time before distractions arise. The basic teaching here is simply to let yourself be aware of everything that passes through your awareness as it is. Don't focus on your thoughts, feelings, and sensations, but don't try to suppress them, either. Just observe them as they come and go.

Anything can arise within space. Thoughts, feelings, and sensations are like birds flying in the sky, which don't leave any trace of their flight.

Let them fly. Let them come and go without a trace.

Let yourself become the space that welcomes any experience without judgment.

That is who you are, after all.

TWELVE

Putting It Together

Mindfulness of Dharma borders on a more advanced practice, known in Sanskrit as *vipaśyanā* and in Tibetan as *lhaktong,* both of which may be translated as "clear seeing" or "seeing things as they truly are." Particularly in Western cultures, both translations have been shortened into a single word, *insight*: a term that recalls the image of my father turning his palms inward to demonstrate the capacity of the mind to look inward at itself—a process through which we begin to realize emptiness as an actual experience rather than as an interesting or instructive concept.

When we begin practicing mindfulness, we're simply noticing. In a sense, we're like a shopkeeper taking inventory of items in his store: "This is here, this is here, this is not here, this is here. . . ." Except that we're a little bit gentler in our noticing. We try, at least, to notice the excess or absence of physical sensations, emotions, and thoughts without judgment.

Through this simple act of noticing, however, an extraordinary transformation begins to occur. Slowly but surely, we begin to let go of the attachments and fixations that keep us locked into identifying with whatever patterns define our experience. As we bring our attention to thoughts, feelings, and physical sensations, we also train our awareness to settle a bit, providing us with an opportunity to glimpse some gaps and to experience the background of space against which the various clouds that occupy our thoughts, feelings, and physical sensations appear.

DEEP EXPERIENCE

When we bring insight into our practice, however, we enter a deeper process of transformation, engaging in a kind of dialogue with our experience.

For example, when we notice some tightness in an area of the physical body, we can begin to break that tightness down into constituent parts. We can look at the body as a construction of little pieces rather than as one big lump. We can explore the thoughts and emotions that contribute to that tightness. Or we can work the other way, looking at the thoughts that incite emotional responses which, in turn, provoke physical sensations. We can also look at the emotions that charge our thoughts and provoke physical sensations.

Whichever means through which we approach mindfulness, we're bound to recognize habitual patterns: lump-like formations of thoughts, feelings, and physical sensations that, upon closer examination, aren't as lumpy as they initially seem.

We can begin to see how these patterns unfold against the background of space. In so doing, we begin to release "I"dentification with them. We start to recognize that long-held patterns aren't as solid as they seem. They aren't an intrinsic part of what we believe to be "I" but rather a series of transitory, interconnected events that contribute to a sense of "I."

The process of dissolving habitual patterns takes some time—maybe an entire lifetime. It doesn't, however, involve distancing or detaching ourselves from our experiences or berating ourselves for bursts of complex emotional, intellectual, or physical events. Rather, it involves a process of extending a sense of experiential realization of the potential from which patterns emerge.

Smile at your patterns. Welcome them in the way you'd welcome a partner, spouse, roommate, or child who barges through the front door while you're in the middle of some other task. Instead of grumbling about the interruption, acknowledge their presence kindly, politely, and perhaps even with a bit of humorous affection. "Hello, honey. Welcome back. I can't join you right now, though. I can't follow you from room to room." Offer them space to move around as they will, while recognizing that *they* are not *you* and *you* are not *them*.

Vipaśyanā or *lhaktong* is often described as "inquiry," an analytical process through which we break down our experiences into their different parts until we see that they're not solid, permanent, or true. But, at least the way I was taught, this inquiry isn't an intellectual process but rather an experimental, experiential one.

Whenever a difficult or challenging experience arises—such as anxiety, panic, jealousy, anger, or physical pain—we can bring all four mindfulness practices together to function as a team.

SPACE IN THE BODY

It's usually easiest to start off practicing what might be called "Team Mindfulness" with Mindfulness of Body. Locate in the body where you feel something most intensely. Notice it; allow yourself to become fully alert to it. Then allow yourself to experience a bit of space, of openness within the body. Reach within your awareness to feel the space around you merging with the body and then rest within that experience.

With practice, merging internal and external space can create a sense of lightness, of floating. Allow yourself to experience that lightness, like feathers floating in the breeze or leaves fluttering in the wind. That lightness not only soothes some of the physical sensations you may be feeling but also helps to dissolve the "glue" that maintains your "I"dentification with your physical body and to break down some of the stories that bind you to your frozen, solid sense of "I."

EMOTIONAL SPACE

Next, look at the subtle body aspect that may be contributing to that physical sensation. Maybe the *tsa* are twisted; maybe the *lung* is stuck. So spend a few moments practicing Mindfulness of Feeling, identifying the emotional component of an experience, talking to your *tsa* and using the vase breathing technique to draw *lung* down to its home place and let it settle.

You might begin by trying to find some area that is a little blocked and admitting a little space there. Some people find it easier to focus more on the center of emotional warmth in their hearts—whether it be love for their children, their spouses, or someone else—and then extend that open warmth to the sensation around the heart and really drop into the unconditional love, letting go of the "I." Within the center of that place, bring the space within the feeling.

The image that comes to mind as I describe this is one of a plastic bag of flour that, at least in days past, people were allowed to carry in their airplane luggage. During the trip, the bag, and the flour within it, would become very tightly compressed as whatever air it may have contained was completely sucked out—"vacuum-packed" is the correct term, I'm told. After disembarking, some people would open the bag and let the air flow back in, allowing both the bag and the flour within it to resume their natural contours.

Similarly, when we work with introducing space into the subtle body, we open up the tight space, first releasing its compression and then using the methods described earlier to breathe into the patterns a sense of relief and release.

SPACIOUS MIND

In almost all cases, at least half of whatever pain or other disturbance we're experiencing is exacerbated by agitated, stuck, or misplaced *lung*. So when we work to bring *lung* down to its home base, or at least closer to it, we may begin to feel an easing of whatever is troubling us—at least enough to look at the mental aspect of the situation: the thoughts that believe "this anxiety is true," "this pain is true," "my thoughts are a part of me."

By practicing Mindfulness of Thought as part of the team, we also begin to get a sense of the validity of our thoughts. Some thoughts, of course, are quite reasonable. If you see flames shooting up your bedroom wall in the middle of the night, it is entirely valid to think, "I'd better get out of here now."

Other thoughts may not be so accurate, such as judgments about our appearance, our competence, or our self-worth. So many such thoughts circulate through our awareness, bits of residue remaining after challenging or even traumatic experiences. But when we begin to question their validity, when we begin to acknowledge the gaps that appear between and among thoughts, we begin to admit a little bit of space among the ideas we believed were solid.

As we deepen our inquiry, we're not only sharpening our awareness but also admitting more space by breaking down the experience into its physical, emotional, and mental elements, dissolving the fixation or solidity of the layers of "I" that keep us locked into a particular feeling or point of view or mood. We're also generating kindness toward ourselves by actually working with a pattern instead of surrendering to its pressure or trying to push it away. Through that application of kindness and gentleness toward ourselves, we're actually beginning to get in touch with the basic warmth of unconditional love.

DROPPING IT

The final step in the Team Mindfulness process is dropping the inquiry altogether and simply resting in the openness and clarity of space. We can accomplish this either by turning our awareness inward to the mind that is aware of all these different aspects of experience or by practicing that little gesture of raising the arms while inhaling and then letting them drop in our laps with an exhalation—and just let all the thoughts, feelings, and physical sensations float there in openness.

Chances are, though, that whatever patterns we've been breaking through using Team Mindfulness will reassert themselves again almost immediately after we've dropped the inquiry. Allowing these patterns to emerge is another, perhaps subtler way of "dropping." The next time they arise, we'll be a little bit wiser, a little bit more welcoming.

Chances are also good that we'll experience a little less intensity in the strength of our patterns. They might be only 5 or 10 percent less powerful, but it's a start. We've seen into the nature of our patterns and they have begun to loosen their hold on us, allowing our own inner warmth to rise up and meet us partway. We can start the process right away again, if we want (and we may be surprised to find that the location of greatest physical intensity may have shifted), and then drop it again. Or we can get up, do something else for a while, and come back to the process a little later.

DIFFERENT DOORWAYS

It's also possible to start from a different doorway, so to speak. Maybe the thoughts "I'm panicking," "I'm so mad," "I've got to get this done today" are the impetus that propels us to engage in Team Mindfulness. So we look, using Mindfulness of Thought—examining a thought, checking its validity, and finding the gaps. Then we turn to Mindfulness of Body to see where this thought or collection of thoughts has affected us most intensely on a physical level, noting it, maybe bringing in a little awareness of all the muscles, nerves, and so on in that location. Then work with the subtle body to draw the *lung* back and down from the area where it may be stuck in a particularly twisted net of *tsa*.

As we grow more familiar with Team Mindfulness, we may find it easier to begin working first with the subtle body. Find some area that is a little blocked. Perhaps we might be aware of some tension around the heart area and commence by extending our awareness there, surrounding it with the kind of intelligent, welcoming warmth we've practiced earlier. At the same time, we can introduce some space into and around it.

Just breathe into the tight place. Breath is both a physical and a subtle manifestation of space. Breathing induces a sense of openness and relaxation that allows our inner warmth to swell, in a similar way that air feeds a small and timid fire, allowing it to grow stronger, brighter, and hotter.

GOING SLOWLY

For most of us, the patterns we've developed during our lives—which, in many ways, are supported by the cultures in which we're very strongly and deeply embedded—are not going to be dissolved in one practice session, or ten, or a hundred. Sometimes it takes years of effort to develop the kind of wisdom that transcends intellect, that simply and clearly recognizes the transitory, unfixed nature of our patterns. It's important, too, to remember that our experiences are shaped by many different patterns—so it's going to take some time to untangle them all.

I urge you, therefore, to refrain from criticizing yourself if you don't experience immediate results—or when you find yourself chasing after thoughts, succumbing to strong emotions, or unable to discover a half second of space. Your intention to practice, to reconnect with your inner spark, is, in itself, a monumental step. On some level, you've made a decision to awaken, and that decision will carry you through many challenging times.

I also encourage you to proceed slowly. The wonderful teachers who guided me through my first steps in mindfulness practice were very careful to say that the most efficient approach when first starting out was to practice for very short periods many times a day. Otherwise, they warned, I'd run the risk of growing bored or disappointed with my progress and eventually give up trying altogether.

This instruction is summed up in one of the Buddha's teachings, which, roughly translated, goes like this: "Drip by drip, a jug gets filled."

It was an analogy drawn on practical observation. During rainy seasons in certain parts of Asia, rain drips through leaky roofs. It's often necessary to place a bowl or some other container under the leak, and soon enough the container is filled and has to be emptied or replaced.

Similarly, when your jugs, bowls, or other containers are filled, empty them. When you first start out, don't set yourself a lofty goal of sitting down to meditate for twenty minutes. Aim instead for ten minutes or even five minutes—utilizing those few moments when you find yourself willing or even desiring just to take a break from the daily grind to observe your mind rather than drifting off into daydreams. Practicing "one drip at a time," you'll find yourself slowly but gradually becoming free of the patterns that are the source of fatigue, disappointment, anger, and despair, and discover within yourself an unlimited source of clarity, wisdom, peace, and compassion.

As you do so, you'll eventually discover that you're ready to begin an even deeper process of reconnecting with the spark within you.

THIRTEEN

Into Action

As we work with the various practices of mindfulness and use them together as a team, a genuine transformation begins to occur. The "solid I" becomes more fluid, and we begin to reconnect with that sense of openness and warmth of essence love that was available to us on the level of the "mere I." At the same time, because we're beginning to come back into balance on the subtle body level and to experience, perhaps for the first time in a long while, a sense of well-being, energy, and inspiration, the "precious I" begins to melt, along with the "social I" through which we define or measure ourselves according to the reactions of other people.

Unfortunately, many of us get caught up in this sense of well-being and forget the most essential lesson that the Buddha—as well as many great teachers of other traditions—tried to instill in us as the deepest of all teachings: that until all of us are free, none of us are free. We rest in our own comfort zones, our contentment dimming our awareness of the pain and hardship that others around us may be feeling.

I recently heard a story, for example, about a woman who advertised herself as a *bodhisattva*—a person who has achieved the great love and openness associated with *bodhicitta*. One night, someone in great physical pain called her and asked if she could drive her to the nearest hospital, which was some distance away from her own house and that of the *bodhisattva*.

"I'm sorry," the *bodhisattva* replied, "but I'm very busy tonight. I'll pray for you, though."

I never learned whether her prayers were effective or not. But her response wasn't that of a true *bodhisattva*. A *bodhisattva*, in the Tibetan Buddhist tradition, is considered a "hero" or "warrior" who is dedicated to bringing to all beings the same freedom he or she has experienced. They are heroes of compassion, going out of their way to assist others in moments of darkness and despair.

I can't really blame this advertised *bodhisattva*, though, because there was a time in my life when I was just as willing to settle into my own comfort zone—a cozy complacency that I ultimately found quite disturbing.

THE LESSON OF A LEAF

Though practice, study, and teaching had helped me to break down some of the problematic attachments to various layers of "I," a few years back I began to feel uncomfortable. After reflecting for a while, I realized that I was caught up in a stage of practice that I've learned to describe as "cozy Dharma," or "cozy realization." It's a stage at which one feels a little bit proud of one's understanding and superficially content with one's accomplishments—where one thinks, "Oh, the Dharma is so good. I'm so happy." Yet lurking underneath that complacency is a nagging discontent, a feeling that the Dharma offers something much grander and more fulfilling than coziness.

I happened to be teaching in Bodhgaya at the time, the place where the Buddha had attained his full understanding of the suffering of living beings and the means to alleviate it. It's a very powerful place, an area of the world that exerts an influence that can induce you to reexamine your life.

As I looked back over my life, my practice, what I'd learned as a student, what I was teaching others, as well as my relationships with my family and friends, I began to sense that something was missing. Yes, I'd managed a way to reconnect with my basic spark and had taught the methods of doing so to thousands of students, but my "hero's heart," the real essence of *bodhicitta*, was only half awake. I'd recognized in myself—while teaching, for example—a tendency to get tired, a feeling of "Oh, I'd like to finish this up soon. I'd like to go here, I'd like to go there. I'd like to be doing something else, go to a movie or rest." I felt the same unrest while conducting the work involved in organizing, building, and repairing monasteries, nunneries, and retreat centers. Even my meditation sessions had become a bit tiresome. I just wanted to sit back, relax, and eat or watch television with my wife and daughters.

I was tired, distracted, and sometimes bored.

But in Bodhgaya, which offers few distractions, I began to think about the many great teachers who had helped and encouraged me. They never seemed to be tired; their enthusiasm for whatever project in which they were engaged never flagged. Maybe they'd get tired physically, but they never lost the strength inside to keep going.

When I looked at my own life, I realized I was losing inner strength because I wasn't completely committed to the goal of absolute *bodhicitta*. I was just locked in my coziness—making boundaries between my work life, my practice life, and my family life. Even though I'd broken through various layers of self, I realized there was another layer to break through: a layer of spiritual coziness, cozy Dharma, cozy compassion, cozy being.

So one evening, after I'd finished my teachings, I went to the area of Bodhgaya that includes a number of ancient shrines and temples, as well as a tree grown from a cutting of the Bodhi tree. I didn't tell any-one where I was going. I just went by myself, with the determination to take a vow to work selflessly for the benefit of all beings, to break be-yond the level of complacency through which I'd allowed myself to continue to do things as long as they made me happy.

It was about sunset, a time that particularly resonates with me as a moment of tenderness. The day is almost done, but there is still light, a poignant moment of transition between the clarity of daylight and the confusion of darkness, a moment in which reality appears to shift, to transform.

I sat under the Bodhi tree and prayed a little bit, then I circumam-bulated it three times while reciting the *bodhisattva* vow, which, in a distilled form, goes something like this: "From now on, until I attain complete freedom from pain and suffering, I dedicate myself wholly and completely, without personal reward, to work for the benefit of all sentient beings." I determined that I would really take on the *bodhisattva* commitment from the depths of my heart.

Just at the moment I completed the vow, I felt something lightly glancing off my head. I opened my eyes and saw at my feet a leaf from the Bodhi tree.

What happened next was quite surprising. I'd been aware of people on either side of me, near the Bodhi tree. I thought they were chanting or praying—but they'd actually been waiting for a leaf to fall. It's illegal to cut a leaf from the tree (otherwise it would just be bare branches). No one can collect a leaf unless it falls naturally.

Suddenly, from all around, people began crowding in, grabbing for the fallen leaf. I have to confess, I felt a similar desire to pick up the leaf and claim it for myself; and since it had fallen right in front of me, I grabbed it. All of this happened in the space of a few seconds. I was hold-ing the leaf, thinking, "I won! The Bodhi tree had sent a leaf to me, and now I have it. I must be such a good person, such a good practitioner!"

As I walked away, though, I began to feel quite guilty. "You're such a lazy *bodhisattva*," I told myself. "You took a vow to dedicate your life to all sentient beings, but you can't give up this leaf to someone else. You're still holding on to it, you're still cherishing it, you're still clinging to the idea of receiving some special sign or blessing." I felt so sad and angry I almost ripped up the leaf and threw it to the ground.

Then another voice came, from nowhere: "Keep this leaf as a reminder of how easy it is to break the commitment to work for the benefit of others. You might say the words as sincerely as you can, but it's your actions that really count—that really determine whether or not you're clinging to coziness, to self-importance, to separateness."

A few days later, I asked one of my students to put the leaf in a frame, along with a line or two I'd written about the experience. I brought the framed leaf back to my home in Nepal and hung it on the wall of the staircase going from the first level up to my bedroom, so I could remind myself every night as I went up to bed and every morning as I came downstairs to start my day of my commitment and how easy it is to break it.

After a month or so, I realized that maybe the placement wasn't so good (it's easy to avoid looking at the wall while going up and down the stairs). Ultimately my wife—who is so much wiser than I in many ways—hung the leaf and my note over our bed. So when I'm at home, it's always over my head when I go to sleep at night and when I wake in the morning. It is as much a part of my dreams as of my waking life.

When I see this framed leaf, I'm reminded that nurturing the spark of being involves two related efforts. The first, of course, entails connecting with our basic openness, intelligence, and warmth. The second necessitates extending the potential we've discovered within ourselves outward into the ways in which we conduct ourselves with everyone and everything we encounter in our daily lives.

So many civilizations have fallen because people have chosen to remain within their own comfort zones, preferring to shore up their own sense of security while ignoring the plight of others. Some, however, have understood the importance of supporting people they may never know. These are examples of people who have demonstrated through their own actions the type of conduct encouraged by people in many different cultures across many different eras. These include ancient religious figures, such as Jesus, Moses, and Muhammad—who all stressed charity and kindness to others. We might also consider more recent figures, like Rosa Parks—often referred to as "the first lady of civil rights"—whose refusal to give up her seat to a white passenger on a bus in Montgomery, Alabama, is seen by many as the act that precipitated the American civil rights movement and opened up a cultural dialogue about treating one another with respect and dignity. We might also consider a young Tunisian man, Mohamed Bouazizi, who set himself on fire to protest unemployment, poverty, and government corruption—a sacrifice that ushered in an unprecedented era of freedom for millions across the Middle East.

BODHICITTA AS A PRACTICE

It has been described earlier that once we connect with essence love, various practices—*tonglen*, for example—can help us to grow that connection into a boundless love that includes all sentient beings. But that is only the second step in our journey. The next step involves actively taking up relative *bodhicitta* as a practice. And that means practicing compassion—which, in turn, involves doing things that you don't really want to do, simply because it will benefit someone else. Few people teach this aspect, preferring instead to describe compassion as empathy—a sympathetic response to the suffering of others. As far as descriptions go, that's not too far off the mark. But, as I was taught, compassion is not just a feeling; it's an action. When Rosa Parks refused to give up her seat, she was acting compassionately. When Mahatma Gandhi undertook a hunger fast to protest foreign occupation of his country, he was acting compassionately. When Mohamed Bouazizi set himself on fire, he was acting compassionately on behalf of all Tunisians.

Were any of them moved by the phrase "relative *bodhicitta*"? I doubt they'd even heard the term. But their actions were motivated by a willingness to endure hardship on the behalf of others, which is the basis of relative *bodhicitta*: Do what needs to be done, even if you don't want to, even if it causes you hardship or pain.

The difference between boundless love and *bodhicitta* is that in boundless love we kind of split our focus doing things for people that may improve their lives, but we also enjoy a secret pleasure in helping that other person—a self-congratulatory sense that we've done something really nice and that we're a better person for doing so. Whatever measure of joy we've offered a person—maybe something such as giving just a smile to a bank teller or a crossing guard—is reflected back to us: "Hey, I did something nice today! What a nice person I am!" We enjoy the joy we bring to others.

Bodhicitta, on the other hand, is an effort to remove any kind of suffering without anticipating the same sort of self-satisfying return.

For example, as one student recently said, "I know my old uncle is living alone. I dread calling him because I know that he's just going to say the same things he said last week and the week before and the week before that. But I call him anyway because it's one of his few contacts with the outside world. Lots of times my response is just 'mhm-mhm, mhm-mhm.' And he takes forever to say good-bye, which infuriates my boyfriend, who wants to see me hang up after the first good-byes. But the poor guy is so lonely I just can't hang up on him."

Another person I know was asked to sit with his mother during a long hospital stay because no one else in his family lived close enough to do so. He hated hospitals—the antiseptic smells, the bland food—but he stayed. Some of the nurses said very nice things to him. "You're such a good son." "You're such a good boy." Once he shot back, "I'm sixty years old, I'm not a BOY!"

But then one nurse came into the room and, after watching him for a moment, said, "You're not doing what you want to do but what you need to do."

"What the hell does that mean?" he asked.

She waited for a moment, but didn't step back at his angry tone.

"You're sitting here, not because you want to but because you believe it's the right thing to do," she said. "Believe me, I've been a nurse for a lot of years and I can see the difference. You're not just sitting by the bed. You're not calling us every five minutes because your mom is in pain. You're sitting here watching her because there's no one else to do it."

She paused for a moment before asking, "You don't know how much heart that takes, do you?"

Then she left the room.

He never saw her again.

Was she an illusion? A messenger? Or just on a temporary assignment?

We'll never know.

But after that, the man described himself as "shaken."

"Someone, somewhere, knew that I was just doing my duty," he said. "I didn't like it, I didn't want it, but it was what I had to do."

That is the essence of *bodhicitta*, fulfilling your responsibilities to others even when you don't want to.

My younger daughter used to cry every time I left home to go off somewhere to teach. When she was younger, I'd hold her in my lap and tell her that I was doing important work that would make a happier, more peaceful place. Now she accepts it a little more gracefully. I miss her when I'm away from Nepal; I miss watching her grow up. I miss my wife terribly. But their acceptance of my absence and of the work I do helps tremendously. They've really understood the meaning of compassion, that in many cases it involves a lot of travel, and staying in places that are strange and sometimes uncomfortable.

This doesn't mean, of course, that practicing *bodhicitta* is completely joyless. The actions we perform may be uncomfortable at first, but as we continue a kind of confidence and strength begins to grow inside us—the full blossoming of essence love, which is utterly lacking in self-involvement, an openness and connectedness with others we never dreamed possible.

In the Buddhist tradition, the active effort of relative *bodhicitta* involves the application of what is known in Sanskrit as *pāramitā* and in Tibetan as *pa-rol-tu-chin-pa*. Both terms are often translated as "perfections," in the sense of being the most open, kind, and intelligent qualities that we can cultivate on the path toward absolute *bodhicitta*. A more literal translation means "going beyond" or "crossing to the other shore"—that "other shore" being the experience beyond the "solid I," beyond the distinction of "self" and "other," beyond conditional love and its complications.

Let's consider them one by one before considering how they can work together, like the practices of mindfulness, as a team.

GENEROSITY

The first *pāramitā*, known in Sanskrit as *dāna* and in Tibetan as *jinpa*, is most frequently translated as "generosity." Traditionally, generosity is divided into three different types.

The first type of generosity is fairly easy to understand. It involves giving material assistance, like food or money. There's an old Buddhist story that in one of his earlier incarnations, the Buddha gave up his body to a starving tigress who couldn't feed her cubs—he willingly let himself be eaten so that the tigress and her cubs could live. I'm fairly certain that if the story is true, the experience must have been rather unpleasant. Whether true or not, it remains as an example of the type of willingness to endure personal hardship on behalf of others.

I would hazard a guess that few of us today are asked by starving tigresses to give up their bodies. But in my estimation, it's a great object lesson in providing food for people who are starving. All around the world, groups of people gather in lines to accept charitable donations of breakfast and lunch for themselves and their children: hungry tigers and tigresses who only want to help their cubs survive.

A global crisis of poverty and starvation has been met to some degree with a generous response. Sometimes this response is met by charitable organizations. Sometimes it is met by governments. After tornadoes ripped through Joplin, Missouri, the government of the United Arab Emirates—a country thousands of miles away from this North American city—pledged up to a million dollars in aid to children whose homes and schools were destroyed. Sometimes it is met by individuals who take time out of their own schedules to shop for groceries or make dinner for a housebound person, as one of my students does on a regular basis for an elderly woman in his apartment building.

"Maybe I'm not being completely generous in the true sense of self-less giving here," he confessed. "The lady is ninety-nine years old! And the stories she can tell about living through changes in the world are amazing. Imagine living through a time of horse-drawn carriages, the first cars, the first airplanes, the first televisions, and something as completely incomprehensible to her as the Internet. 'What's this Facebook I hear about?' she asks. 'What's this Twitter? Seems like a lot of nonsense to me. In my day we wrote letters. We made telephone calls. It was all so personal then. Seems like now the people are getting less personal.'

"Okay, maybe she repeats her complaints sometimes, and since she's practically deaf, she does talk a little loudly. She tries to keep me in her apartment as long as she can, just for company's sake, I guess. And that's a little irritating because I have to get up early to get to work. But I worry about her. I care about her. I want to make sure that she has enough food and that she eats and that she has a little company. If that means I go without a few extra hours of sleep, okay."

I was taught that the first kind of generosity could extend beyond material assistance to giving emotional sustenance. Sometimes this means offering comfort or encouragement to someone who's having a difficult day, a difficult week, month, or—as many people across the globe have experienced—a difficult year, a difficult decade, a difficult life. In the past few years alone, we've seen an extraordinary outpouring of generosity from people in response to events that have devastated communities and countries. For example, thousands of people across the world have contributed their time to the citizens of Haiti after the disastrous earthquake in 2010.

Many people who give so generously don't identify themselves as Buddhists. They're giving because it's their nature to give. Seen in this light, it's possible that the Buddha codified generosity as a practice in order to arouse a potential rooted within our own nature, the spark of warmth and openness that enables us to connect with our own hearts and the hearts of others.

A student recently mentioned that she was brought up by parents who were raised during the Great Depression of the 1930s and had learned from them a hard lesson in "pinching pennies."

"But the more I think about it," she said, "the more I think that the Great Depression was not just an economic thing. The Great Depression, like the recession of today, was an emotional thing, an expression of a loss of confidence in ourselves.

"So I just feel good when I can give a few dollars to a friend," she continued. "I feel connected, like we're all in this—whatever *this* is—together."

The second type of generosity involves offering protection to those whose lives are threatened in some way. There are many individuals who engage in this kind of activity, offering assistance to people who are about to lose their homes, their cars, even their children. They offer drug and alcohol addicts the opportunity to enter rehabilitation facilities to detoxify from the poisons in their systems and, in some cases, learn skills that will help them to acquire jobs. Shelters that protect women and children who have been abused in various ways offer a kind and caring environment that provides a basis for these women and children to overcome their fears and their histories of abuse. A group known as Doctors Without Borders has dedicated untold resources to people in a number of countries to receive medical and psychological treatment, offering a haven of safety.

The final aspect of generosity involves offering understanding. Usually this involves giving a Dharma teaching, such as the type given to large groups of students by the great masters of the Buddhist tradition. But there's also a way of offering understanding that is, in itself, quite generous—as exemplified by an encounter I had with Dilgo Khyentse

Rinpoche several years ago in Bodhgaya, at the same time I was becoming an accidental teacher.

Rinpoche was giving a massive set of teachings to more than a thousand people over the course of several weeks. During that period, a friend of mine, a fellow *tulku* from Tashi Jong, approached me with a little bit of a problem. He would be going into retreat in a few months and needed a special teaching from Rinpoche—a teaching that I was also interested in receiving. But we thought, "Wow, he's so busy. He spends his whole day teaching all these people, he probably won't have any time for us."

But having met Dilgo Khyentse Rinpoche on a few occasions at Tashi Jong and other places, I knew how kind he was. So, I thought, "Well, it can't hurt to ask." So one day, during lunchtime, I sort of snuck in to where he was eating. I wasn't terribly surprised, given Rinpoche's free and relaxed style, to see that his door was open— though meals are usually considered "private times," when a teacher can relax a little bit. Rinpoche saw me standing near the door and invited me in. Suddenly I felt quite shy about asking him for a favor; but I realized that ultimately he would say either "yes" or "no."

He didn't even pause after I asked. The request was barely out of my mouth when he replied, "Come tomorrow during lunchtime."

The next day, my friend and I went to Rinpoche's room, and he gave us the teaching we requested with the same depth of detail and attention with which he was giving his public teachings, without any conditions. He didn't ask for donations or gifts. He didn't care about our status as *tulkus*. He didn't rush through anything. He didn't just cut to the essential points. He gave himself totally to explaining the teachings in great detail and making sure we understood them.

That was actually a very powerful lesson for me in terms of developing my own teaching style. Whenever a student asks for a special teaching in private, I remember Dilgo Khyentse Rinpoche's generosity, and I try to emulate his example by giving as complete a teaching as I can, without any other consideration except helping whoever comes to me to better understand and practice the Dharma.

Generosity in teaching can also be passed down a little bit more casually. For instance, one student who began working for a large international corporation was disturbed by the volatile reactions of her boss.

"Don't take it personally," her coworker told her. "He's afraid about his job, and he can't help but pass that fear to you. Whatever he says, though, whatever he does, has nothing to do with you.

"Give the guy some love," he said. "He's wicked scared."

DISCIPLINE

How do you love someone who is scared and who scares you?

By practicing the second *pāramitā*, known in Sanskrit as *sīla* and in Tibetan as *tsultrim*.

The second *pāramitā* is commonly translated as "ethics" or "morality"—although I've heard it translated as "moral discipline" or simply as "discipline." In its most basic sense, this sort of discipline means refraining from behaviors and tendencies that are harmful to others or to oneself. Traditionally, such behaviors are divided into three categories: physical actions, such as killing, stealing, and abusive sexual behavior; activities of speech, such as lying, slander, harsh words, and frivolous or what is sometimes called "useless" speech; and mental or emotional tendencies, which include greed and malice.

The harmful mental tendencies also include holding what are often referred to as "wrong views"—which, in the Buddhist tradition, can encompass a number of ideas. Most simply, perhaps, "holding wrong views" refers to holding something as true which is not true. In the preceding pages, we have come to see how much pain and confusion is generated in our own experience when we hold certain ideas about ourselves. We've also seen how limited our choices become when we see our patterns as true. So practicing discipline involves continually working to find space in our patterns, to find the gaps in the images we hold about ourselves. It also means finding the gaps in our ideas about others, releasing images that we hold about a manager, a coworker, a friend, or a partner.

For example, it's easy to judge someone who is often tense or angry and to become defensive around him or her, creating all sorts of stories that we might share with others in the form of gossip. Practicing discipline in this case means stepping back and trying to look with a bit more objectivity at the reasons the person may be angry or tense. Perhaps he or she is constantly being criticized by someone higher up and is afraid of getting fired. Maybe that person is dealing with someone who is seriously ill. Perhaps he or she is caught up in a difficult relationship. So when we think about others, when we evaluate their behavior and respond to it, we strive to see past the immediate to offer them the same space, the same kindness, we've learned to offer ourselves.

Discipline also involves cultivating behaviors and attitudes that are beneficial to others and to oneself. Such behaviors and attitudes are typically understood as opposites of the harmful activities described above. Instead of killing, we work to preserve life; rather than steal, we give (practicing generosity). We tell the truth. We say kind things about people. We strive to speak gently. We think about what we can do for others, rejoice in their accomplishments and achievements, and strive to understand their behavior in terms of temporary causes and conditions.

Regardless of our approach—refraining from harmful activities or pursuing beneficial ones—the essence of discipline means cultivating a wide heart and a broad understanding that allows us to forgive ourselves and others for the mistakes we've made under the influence of "I."

To use an example, several years ago an aged monk traveled from Tibet to India to see a great teacher. While they were talking, the monk mentioned that he'd been imprisoned for a number of years after the Cultural Revolution.

"I was so scared," the old monk said.

"Of dying?" the teacher asked him. "Of being beaten? Tortured?"

The old man shook his head.

"No, no," he whispered. "I was scared of losing love for the men who guarded the prison. They had guns and clubs. They threatened us all the time. But so many of them were just obeying orders. They had wives and children and parents to protect. So they beat us and killed us to protect their families.

"I was scared that I would forget that these men were treating us badly because they wanted to protect their families. They were scared for the people they loved.

"And I'm scared because I don't feel much sympathy for them anymore. I feel sometimes that I want to hurt them as much as they hurt me and hurt the people I loved."

His fear, as the teacher pointed out, was the measure of his love. If he'd surrendered to these thoughts and feelings, he might have been trapped in the pattern of the "solid I," seen threats in the "solid other," and engaged in all sorts of "precious" stories about himself and his situation.

That is the real meaning of discipline: maintaining love, maintaining the hope that every living being will awaken, even in the most difficult or challenging conditions.

The deepest lesson in discipline is one I learned from my father.

Before I set off to America to begin the first of my teachings there, I visited my father's little room in Nagi Gompa and asked for advice on how to teach to this new audience. His answer was surprising.

Giving a little secret smile, he said, "Don't let the praise go to your head. People will compliment you. They'll say how great you are, how wonderful your teachings are. Accept these compliments graciously, but let them go. Whatever compliments your students give you have nothing to do with you. They're really a reflection of the truth and power of the Dharma. How you teach is not important. *What* you teach *is*.

"Oh, I know," he continued, "you're approaching a new world. You want to be modern. I don't blame you, my son. The world changes, but the Dharma doesn't change. It's as true now as it was two thousand years ago. Just don't let your way of teaching make you think you're anyone special. What the Buddha taught has endured for centuries."

He then went on to explain that many teachers can get caught up in what may best be described as a "personality problem"—a phenomenon I've witnessed myself over the past several years. Students become attracted by a particular teacher's style, his or her charisma, and the teacher may come to think of himself or herself as special.

"What's really special," my father said, smiling more broadly, "is the teaching itself, the Dharma.

"No matter what you become publicly, don't let yourself be carried away by praise. People will say nice things about you. They'll tell you what a great teacher you are. Don't let the clouds take you over."

As looked out his window, the sky was already darkening.

"It's tempting, I know," he said. "People call me great. But my true purpose in life is not to be great, or famous, but to teach the Dharma as best I know how—which is very little. Remember how little you know. Remember how much you have to learn. That will keep you humble. And humbleness is the base of discipline. Until you become a buddha, you still have a lot to learn. Remember that you're a simple human being. No matter who you are, remember the spark, remember the essence of your being.

"Oh, there's so much to learn. Open your heart to what people ask you, what people tell you. Only through an open heart can you gain an open mind."

Yes, it's important to keep on practicing even when we don't want to. Yes, it's important to behave toward others with grace and dignity. But the most important aspect of discipline is humility. We may have learned a great deal over the course of the years, but we have to resist the temptation of becoming proud of what we've learned. There's so much we don't know, and so many opportunities to learn more about ourselves and others, and about the relationship between absolute and relative reality and the relationship between emptiness and appearance—the causes and conditions that are the basis of our temporal, or relative, experience.

PATIENCE

The third *pāramitā*—*kṣānti* in Sanskrit and *zöpa* in Tibetan—is often translated as "patience." But how do we practice patience? What are the obvious and subtle meanings of this practice?

Like the two previous *pāramitās*, patience can be understood on several levels. The most obvious is to refrain from our impulse to retaliate against someone who acts angrily or violently toward us. Someone hits us, we want to hit him back. Someone insults us to our face, we want to insult him back. Someone starts spreading gossip behind our back, we feel an urge to spread equally hateful gossip behind his back.

That doesn't mean that we attempt to push down or push away feelings of anger when they arise. For example, if someone doesn't respond to our generosity or says something or does something unpleasant or with which we don't agree, we might experience a flash of anger or fear. Patience, in this case, means that we recognize our angry or fearful response, but we don't act on it. We recognize that someone is causing us pain because he or she is experiencing pain. We don't lash out at someone because we're overtired, uncomfortable, or stressed, and we accept that those around us may be experiencing similar conditions.

A second aspect of patience involves being willing to endure pain and hardship without losing our sense of motivation. We remember that our goal is to help others to experience freedom, kindness, openness, and warmth, and because of that goal we're willing to deal with whatever obstacles come up in the process of accomplishing it. Sometimes practicing this kind of patience involves something as simple as agreeing to take someone to the doctor when we don't necessarily have the time and will have to rearrange our own schedule or perhaps go without an hour or two of sleep. It may mean meditating when we're tired and are tempted to say, "I'll skip it and add a few minutes tomorrow." It may involve a more significant commitment, like making time to visit a chronically ill or aging friend or family member.

I'm sure we can all find situations in our own lives that require extending ourselves beyond our "comfort zones." The point in approaching such activities and situations with patience is to maintain our connection with the desire to be of service, to be the light for someone who feels pressed by darkness, to be the warmth for those who have lost the connection to their own spark. When we maintain our motivation we often find, to our surprise, that we have more energy than we thought; that the hardships or obstacles we face aren't as intense, scary, or prohibitive as they initially appeared. We begin to experience a subtle and inspiring joy in stepping farther away from our "comfort zones."

A third aspect of patience involves accepting the way things are. Many painful events occur in our lives, and nothing we can say or do can change the situation. Over the past few years, I've met quite a few people who lost friends and relatives during the attack on the World Trade Center on September 11. Many of them are angry, understandably so.

"I'm sad, of course," one person said. "Horrified might be a better word. Shocked. I mourn, but I can't allow myself to descend into bitterness. I get that some may, and I respect that. But the best tribute I could give to the husband I lost is to move forward, to live my life as he would have wished to do. I could have spent the past ten years focusing on what I'd lost. But I know he would have hated that. Instead, after a few years I started looking at living again, going out to dinner with friends, and, well, meeting someone new. It took me a while to start dating again. But now I'm engaged. And in the next few months we plan to get married. The man I lost on September 11 was the one of the kindest, gentlest, smartest, best men I've ever known. I don't know if I can arrange to have his picture at my wedding as 'best man,' but I know he'll be there, smiling at us."

DILIGENCE

The fourth *pāramitā* is often translated as "perseverance," "diligence," "energy," "effort," or, sometimes, "zeal." Its basic meaning lies in dedicating ourselves with joy and enthusiasm to our practices and to our aspiration to benefit others. Diligence resembles patience somewhat in terms of cultivating a willingness to bear adversity. But while patience involves not shying away from challenges, diligence implies an active commitment to taking on the challenges that arise when we commit to helping others. Often involving some personal sacrifice of time, energy, and other resources, diligence may sound like a hard road. But *tsondru*, the Tibetan word used to describe this *pāramitā*, and *vīrya*, the Sanskrit word, both imply an invigorating sense of strength, calm, and focus in taking action that help others.

To use an example, a woman I know recently committed several weeks to staying by her aging father's bedside as he passed through the final stages of his life. It's never easy watching someone die, but she stayed by his bedside, holding his hand, talking to him, listening when he was able to speak. At the same time, she worked to soothe her mother, who suffers from obsessive-compulsive disorder and was frantic during those final weeks.

"But," she said, "however emotionally hard it was, my father's final hours were incredibly peaceful. My mother actually sat by his side, holding his hand as he passed. I'm so glad I was able to be there for him and for her."

It's said that diligence is a kind of armor that helps us to face challenging situations—and that is consistent with the image of a *bodhisattva* as a kind of warrior or hero. But we must remember that this kind of warrior or hero is dedicated to awakening and fanning the spark in others. The armor he or she wears is not some sort of mask but an outpouring of light glowing from within.

Diligence also means taking small actions and appreciating the effect of our accomplishments. In my own case, for example, if I want to clean my kitchen I choose a small area to clean—the stove or the table. I clean those areas and then I rest for a few moments (or may be a little bit longer). Then I come back and look at the area that I've cleaned and say, "Wow, this area is really clean. I did a good job." This gives me the energy or enthusiasm to start working on another small area. This is perhaps a different approach from trying to complete a total cleaning, starting a little bit here, moving a little bit there, but never really focusing on one particular area. And appreciating the work that you've done in one small area gives you a kind of enthusiasm for going on to the next area. Without this sort of delight, diligence cannot be developed. We approach our activities with the kind of forcefulness that can make us physically or emotionally tense. We feel, "I have to do this. I have to get this done right now, right away, altogether." And that kind of attitude can provoke physical and emotional stress.

So that's my understanding of the appropriate way of approaching diligence: breaking down a large task into smaller pieces, and then taking a little rest. But the most important part of the process is allowing ourselves a moment or two to really appreciate what we've accomplished. When we do that, our confidence in completing a big task begins to grow. We begin to feel, "Yes, bit by bit I can do this—whatever *this* is."

CONCENTRATION

The fifth *pāramitā*, known in Sanskrit as *dhyana* or sometimes as *samadhi*, and in Tibetan as *samten*, is translated as "concentration." While it is often understood as practicing some type of meditation, the deeper meaning of concentration involves allowing the mind to rest very simply, alertly, and openly. Practicing concentration in a light and easy way can actually help in simplifying decisions that might otherwise seem overwhelmingly complex.

For example, several years ago I attended a long teaching in Tibet offered by Adeu Rinpoche. As in the case of many long teachings, this one was very complex, involving many long periods of chanting religious texts and other ceremonial elements that had to be performed quite precisely. As I watched Adeu Rinpoche, I saw that he observed the whole event very calmly and clearly. He just sat there with his eyes open, doing what he had to do as master of the ceremonial parts of the teaching. He was completely unshakable and steady, not paying any particular attention to what the monks participating in the teaching were doing.

During breaks in the teaching, I heard him criticizing some of the monks, telling them, "No, you made some mistakes."

I was amazed. He didn't appear to be paying any special attention to particular events, yet he was aware of everything. So one day, during a lunch break, I asked him, "How did you know what was happening? I didn't see your eyes wandering, your attention shifting."

"I was in *samadhi*," he replied.

He went on to explain that resting steadily in completely open, spacious attention, there is no block; in practicing *samadhi*, a person could see everything that was happening without having to focus on any particular thing.

"It was like seeing a reflection in a mirror," he explained. "But the mirror is so wide and so steady, you can see whatever is occurring in the room, without any prejudice or bias. You can see everything going on the room, without focusing any particular event.

"You have to trust in space, because space is always there. If you trust in or focus on phenomena, in appearances—which are impermanent and always changing, always jumping around—then you're kind of always fighting with phenomena.

"So you fully trust in the space in which all phenomena appear. When you do that, all your senses are open. Clarity and steadiness come together."

I saw an example of the same sort of calm, steady openness in my father about a year or so before he passed away. It had become apparent that his physical health was deteriorating, so I decided to visit him more often and spend more time with him. At that time, even as his body was failing, he had begun a new program to expand and improve the shrine room at Nagi Gompa, the place where people could pray and meditate. (Actually my father was always engaged in building and expanding. He never got involved with any fund-raising efforts. People just left money as a traditional offering for teachings or blessings, and then one day he'd say, "Oh, there's enough here to build or fix things.")

One of the projects involved housing a very large statue of Tara, the female embodiment of compassion. These statues are considered very precious and are often protected against dust in a sort of cabinet fronted by a glass window. My father asked me to help complete this project, and one day, when I went to check on its progress, I saw that because the statue was so large, the workers who had installed the glass window had had to use two panes of glass. But the two pieces joined exactly at the point of the statue's eyes, so you couldn't really see the eyes at all.

I went upstairs to inform my father about the problem and ask his advice. He was, of course, in his small room where he both slept and gave teachings. The entrance was not closed off by a door but rather by a heavy curtain. I pulled back the curtain a little bit and saw that he was meditating. Not wishing to disturb him, I let the curtain fall back and waited for a few minutes. Then I thought, "Maybe he's finished now," and peeked back in. He was still sitting, calmly and loosely, meditating. I waited and peeked again—maybe four or five times.

After about half an hour I started to get a little bit cold standing in the hallway and began thinking, a bit selfishly, "Well, this is not really my work. It's his monastery, and I'm working for him, so why don't I just go in?" At the same time, I was interested to see how he would respond—whether he would break from his meditative state and pay attention to "practical" concerns or whether, as I'd heard of great masters, his meditation was so open and free that without leaving that state he could respond accurately and precisely to any situation around him.

So I went in, and addressed him formally.

"Rinpoche."

He looked at me calmly without any change in his eyes or expression, no sign of a break between meditating and dealing with an intrusion. I told him about the problem, asked for his advice, and he gave me some instructions. And as I backed out of the room he simply continued sitting calmly. There was no sign that he'd broken his concentration or composure or that he had to reconnect with his practice. There was no in and out. He was the same, whether meditating or giving advice about a construction issue. He was so clear and open, but there was no sense of holding on to that clarity and openness; it was just part of his being, effortless and continuous.

This was a great lesson for me. Addressing my father and listening to his instructions, I realized that concentration is not an effort of focusing on something but an abiding in a spacious, "centerless center" from which to function.

It is also the platform or preparation for the next *pāramitā*.

WISDOM

Finally we come to the sixth *pāramitā*, *prajñā* in Sanskrit and *sherab* in Tibetan, commonly translated as "wisdom."

It's important to note that there are two kinds of wisdom. The first is simply a discriminating capacity, the tendency to wonder, to question, to pull together information, analyze it, and make decisions. Unless we have some physical or genetic damage, we all have this common wisdom, this basic intelligence or ability to distinguish between different phenomena.

We're always analyzing something—measuring the distance between cars, for example, or scanning people around us to determine their moods. Such analysis is often carried out automatically and unconsciously.

The second type of wisdom is referred to as "transcendent wisdom," which is perhaps best understood as the culmination of insight: the ability to see the essentially interdependent, temporary, and illusory nature of relative reality and the fundamentally open, clear, and limitless nature of absolute reality. It's the capacity to distinguish between our fantasies and projections—our "I-stories" and "other stories"—and the way things truly are. It's the keen perception that enables us to see the space beyond the clouds, the unconditional love layered over by habitual patterns of identification and misunderstanding grounded in hope and fear.

At the same time, it's an intuitive recognition that appearances are able to emerge *because* of the background of emptiness; that clouds can be seen to come and go *because* of the background of space; that it is *because* of the cognitive and emotional skills we've gained in our adventures through the various dimensions of "I" that we can reconnect with our essential nature and nurture that spark into a brilliant flame.

So in the practice of transcendent wisdom, we have to connect with the analytical potential of our being and develop it deliberately. We have to recognize that questioning aspect of our minds, that curiosity, that urge to grow and to know.

How do we do that?

Ordinary wisdom—what we may call intellect or intelligence—is colored by prejudice, bias, hope, fear, past experiences, fixation. So when we begin to practice transcendent wisdom, we begin by analyzing the analyzer. We use the meditation practices to sharpen our natural intelligence, to identify our biases, our prejudices, and so on in order to arrive at a more precise understanding of habitual patterns of interpreting experience.

As one student expressed it recently, "It's like learning to look at the world without sunglasses. If you've always worn sunglasses, you can still see, but everything you see is slightly tinted by the color of the sunglasses. Practicing this *pāramitā* is a little bit like taking off your sunglasses. You might not be able to stand the brightness for too long, but oh, the colors you see! Dizzying at first, maybe, but then a kind of curiosity takes over. You begin to want to see those different colors. You want to see what the world looks like when it's not all painted green."

In the same way, we must develop, glimpse by glimpse, some steadiness in transcendent wisdom. First we must recognize it in our own experience and then nurture it through meditation and practice. Once this experience of wisdom has gained some stability, we can use it as a tool to look at the world without sunglasses.

So how do we recognize transcendent wisdom?

Relax. Let your thoughts and feelings come and go and rest in the clarity that emerges when you simply watch without engaging. That's why it's recommended to practice mindfulness and *samadhi* first. When you have achieved a state of calmness and readiness, then you are ready to know, ready to understand in a deep way the dance between emptiness and appearance. Once you catch a glimpse of that dance, don't hang on to it. Just let it go, like your first glimpse of essence love.

WORKING TOGETHER

Of course, in any teaching format—whether oral or written—the *pāramitās* are explained one by one. In actual practice, however, they function together as a team. It takes some diligence to practice patience, for example; some discipline to practice meditation; some wisdom to practice generosity in a way that truly benefits others. In many cases, two or three or more *pāramitās* work together.

For instance, quite recently I was detained in London because of the ash cloud spilling out from the volcano in Iceland. Unfortunately I'm not clairvoyant: Had I booked a flight that departed four hours earlier, I would have been able to fly unhindered to a meditation retreat I was scheduled to lead in California.

I was staying at a small hotel, and for several days—like so many other stranded travelers—I watched the reports on television and listened to announcements that Heathrow Airport would reopen in two hours, four hours, six hours. With every announcement, I'd dutifully take my bags down to the lobby, only to discover that the airport would remain closed for a few more hours; so I'd take my bags back up to my room and wait for the next announcement.

After a few days, I got tired of sitting around waiting and decided to take a walk. As I passed through the lobby, I overheard three women talking. Two of them were complaining about how intolerable the waiting was. The third said, "Well, in this kind of situation, all we can do is wait and watch."

As soon I heard that, I felt a kind of relief—and at the same time thought, "Wow, what a wonderful lesson in the teamwork of *pāramitās* this is!" Acknowledging this situation as it was in a way exemplified wisdom, the recognition that although the condition was serious it was also temporary. Waiting was an example of patience. Watching was the kind of continuity of effort that exemplifies diligence. The woman exhibited a kind of generosity, too, in offering this sane perspective to the other two ladies, and as I strolled out onto the London street, I felt as though I'd benefited from it as well.

Why?

Because in many ways it brought me back to the reasons I continue to teach. It's not always comfortable, traveling around the world nine or ten months out of the year.

It's said that after the Buddha attained enlightenment he didn't believe he could communicate what he'd discovered to others, but that gods and goddesses gathered around him and encouraged him to find the means to reach so many suffering beings, to teach them to reconnect with their spark, to open their hearts and their minds. I assure you, no gods or goddesses visited me in Bodhgaya and asked me to teach—just a friend I'd met at Tashi Jong.

At first I was hesitant, but as more and more people showed up, I saw in them a desire to learn how to heal their emotional wounds, to connect with a spark they felt inside themselves but couldn't quite reach. I wasn't very good at first, but just seeing the hope, the glimmer of understanding on their faces, a subtle relaxation in their bodies, I began to recognize that however incompetent a teacher I was, I was in a position to help these people awaken to the possibilities within themselves, to live fuller, deeper lives and to forge connections with each other and with the world around them for which they longed.

If that means that I have to leave my wife and children for months at a time, so be it. When that leaf from the Bodhi tree fell before me, I came to an understanding: My life is not my own. It belongs to billions of beings who are longing to awaken, to feel more actively and intensely the spark of light and love within themselves.

I do things now that twenty years ago I couldn't have imagined. I travel around the globe. I shift my teachings to suit the people sitting in front of me.

I build bridges and do my best to help people to trust that those bridges will stand.

FOURTEEN

Trust

Trust is perhaps the most important quality needed to comprehend and actually begin to practice the teachings of the Dharma. Trust opens the heart and then offers the possibility of opening the mind.

I learned a very important lesson in trust during my first year at Tashi Jong. Khamtrul Rinpoche was still building the monastery. Part of that building effort involved filling statues with precious objects such as ancient relics and scrolls he'd managed to bring from Tibet to India before they were destroyed. Because I was very short (and, at that time, very thin) I was often asked to crawl into these statues to place these precious objects.

Sometimes, when something was needed, he would ask me to go to his private room and fetch it from a suitcase he'd stored there. I can hardly begin to describe how monumental it was for the head lama of a large monastery to give a twelve-year-old boy the keys to his private room and ask him to retrieve things that had been carried, under great danger, from Tibet to India.

"Wow," I thought, "he trusts me."

Aside from the relics and the scrolls, there was a bit of money in the room—donations from people who wanted to help him build the monastery.

And even though I saw it, I never once considered stealing a little bit of it.

Why?

His trust awakened the essence love within me. I loved him, partly because he was a kind and gentle man. But there was something more. He embodied essence love. He made no distinction between a twelve-year-old boy and a monk who might have been years older and much more reliable. He didn't see any difference. He offered me the same respect, the same kindness that he would offer to an adult. He built bridges of the heart.

I wish I could have learned more from him, but he passed away two years after I entered Tashi Jong. So many teachers took his place in my heart: Tselwang Rindzin, my father, Dilgo Khyentse Rinpoche, and Adeu Rinpoche. I can never repay their kindness, I can only pass on the lessons they taught me about openness, clarity, patience, generosity, and diligence, and the lessons they taught me about building trust in my own capabilities and the importance of sharing that trust with others—to build bridges that cross what appear as obstacles, and to do my best to help others across those bridges.

The importance of trust was reaffirmed at the end of Adeu Rinpoche's first visit to India in 1980. I walked with him to the border between Nepal and China. He'd spent more than a year in India and Nepal, and he was very kind, very open; I felt I could ask him many questions. I'm not a very intellectual person. I don't understand things the first time I hear them, as many other people do. So I constantly ask for clarification, then practice the answers, and, when confused, ask again. Adeu Rinpoche, among all the many teachers I've had the great fortune to meet, was especially patient with my constant questions.

When we reached the border, I began to feel very sad about parting from him. I offered him a *khata*—a white silk scarf symbolizing an offering of the heart—and he gave me a hug.

Then he stepped back and said, "Some things you have to trust." He didn't say, "You're too intellectual, you ask too many questions." He just said, "Some things are very simple. Just do what you've been taught, and the results will follow."

Then he turned and began walking across the border. I watched him until he disappeared beyond the horizon, amazed at his insight into my doubtfulness—but not criticizing it.

"Just trust," he said. "Just do it."

Over the years, as I've practiced what I was taught, I've seen the benefits, and I offer my students the same advice: "Just trust. Just do it."

But there's an important caution implied in this lesson.

THE BOAT

On a few occasions, I've heard a strange proverb repeated by my teachers. Ordinary people don't attain freedom because they *don't* meditate. Practitioners don't attain freedom because they *do* meditate. It took me quite a while to understand the meaning of this statement.

Meditation, conduct, and understanding are all like parts of a beautiful boat that help us cross a kind of river formed by our patterns, our layers of "I," our particular challenges. In order to cross the river, we need to take the boat. But once we get to the other side, no matter how beautiful the boat is or how much we've enjoyed the ride, it's futile to pick it up and carry it on our backs as we continue along our journey. We appreciate it, we feel gratitude toward it, but if we're to continue on, we must leave it behind.

I'm not saying that we should stop practicing but rather that we take time as we proceed along our path to be honest with ourselves. It's so easy to get hooked on the practices, on the spiritual highs, on a sense of breaking through patterns and making some sort of progress, on the pride of doing things correctly. But eventually we have to let all that go. We need to stop doing and simply *be*. We need to simply trust the spark within us.

LETTING GO

Such trust is difficult. It may be accompanied by a bit of joy, perhaps a bit of wistful sadness—maybe a mixture of several different thoughts, feelings, and sensations. Whatever our experience, if we can allow ourselves to simply *be* with that experience and appreciate it, that is the true transformation, the true healing, the true opening of our hearts and minds.

Best of all, when we can allow ourselves to be as we are, we create the space for others to be as *they* are. A sense of confidence begins to open up between us, creating the opportunity for that other person to open up and extend the same sort of trust in another person—like the flame of one candle lighting another, and that candle lighting another, and on and on. That is the essence and the goal of all our meditation, all our practice, all the understanding we bring to the layers of "I": to let it go, to let it pass from one to another to another, to let the love that is within us—that *is* us—to awaken and spread, moment by moment, step by step, river by river, road by road, and bridge by bridge.

We began this journey together with an admission of an embarrassing story about how I, trained in the philosophies and practices of Buddhism, discovered terror in attempting to cross something that appeared invisible, and the humiliation I felt that someone so well-schooled could experience such fear. It was just a bridge, after all, and many were walking across it with admirable aplomb.

Were they all Buddhists?

Probably not.

But they had no fear. They crossed that bridge as if it were just an everyday experience.

At many times in our lives, we arrive at points at which fear, judgment, and past experiences of pain and suffering can obscure our ability to see that so many of the challenges we face, so many of the bridges we must cross, are ones of our own making; that we've developed patterns that shape the ways in which we view and respond to the various events we encounter as we journey through life. The practices offered in the preceding pages are all aimed at reconnecting with the basic spark that resides deep within us. As we reconnect with that spark, it begins to grow brighter and brighter. It becomes a flame through which others can begin to recognize the same brightness, the same warmth and openness, within themselves. When we recognize and open to the spark within us, when we open our hearts and our minds, we allow everyone around us to open up. As we step across whatever bridge we encounter with a sense of confidence and openness, we offer others an opportunity to reach deeply into their own being, to recognize that beyond or behind their present fears and pains there is a memory of a time when they experienced a connectedness, an openness, a warmth; a time before essence love was layered over by cultural conditioning, before we developed solid, precious, and social "I's."

Crossing bridges, discovering patterns, reconnecting with essence love and extending that love to others is a journey that I believe with my whole heart we're all able to make.

Whatever you need to take that first step lies within you. It may seem like a tiny light right now, but with every step you take it will grow stronger and brighter. It will become contagious. As you cross bridges, reconnect with essence love, and begin to recognize the warmth, openness, and clarity within you, you'll inspire others to see the light of love within themselves.

You don't have to say anything. You don't have to teach anything. You just have to be who you are: a bright flame shining in the darkness of despair, a shining example of a person able to cross bridges by opening your heart and opening your mind.

Glossary

absolute *bodhicitta*   Direct insight into the nature of mind. See also application *bodhicitta*, aspiration *bodhicitta*, *bodhicitta*, relative *bodhicitta*.

absolute reality   The indefinable, infinitely open, limitless potential for anything to appear, disappear, change, and reappear. See also emptiness, *tongpa-nyi*.

application *bodhicitta*   Taking steps to cultivate the liberation of all sentient beings from all forms and causes of suffering through recognition of their buddha nature. See also absolute *bodhicitta*, aspiration *bodhicitta*, *bodhicitta*, relative *bodhicitta*.

aspiration *bodhicitta*   Cultivation of the heartfelt desire to raise all sentient beings to the level at which they recognize their buddha nature. See also absolute *bodhicitta*, application *bodhicitta*, *bodhicitta*, relative *bodhicitta*.

bodhicitta   Sanskrit. The "mind" or "heart" of awakening. See also absolute *bodhicitta*, application *bodhicitta*, aspiration *bodhicitta*, relative *bodhicitta*.

bodhisattva   A person who has achieved the great love and openness associated with *bodhicitta*.

buddha nature   The innate, limitless capacity for openness, clarity, and warmth. See also *sugatagarbha* and *tathagatagarbha*.

clarity   The capacity to be aware of all the things we experience, to see the stuff of our experience and to know that we're seeing it. See also *ö-sel-wa*.

compassion   A degree of openness and intelligence that enables us to see the suffering of others and to spontaneously move to help them. See also *nying-jé*.

dak   Tibetan. Self or "I."

dak ché dzin   Tibetan. Literally "grasping the self as precious."

dak tenpar dzin (dak dzin)   Tibetan. Grasping the self or "I" as true; the solid "I."

dak tsam   Tibetan. The "mere I."

dāna   Sanskrit. Tibetan: *jinpa*. Generosity, the first *pāramitā*.

dharma   Sanskrit: The truth, or the way things are; specifically, the teachings of the Buddha.

dhyana   Also known as *samadhi* (Sanskrit) and *samten* (Tibetan). Concentration, the fifth *pāramitā*.

drenpa   Tibetan. The aspect of consciousness that draws attention to an object.

dzin   Tibetan. Grasping or fixation.

dzogchen   Tibetan. The Great Perfection, a combination of two words: *dzog*, a contraction of the noun *dzogpa*, which does, on a primary level, mean "perfect" or "perfection," and *chen*, which means "great" or "vast." *Dzogpa*, on a secondary level, means "including everything."

emptiness   The inherently indescribable basis of all phenomena from which anything and everything arises. See also *śūnyatā*.

enlightenment   In Buddhist terms, the firm and unshakable recognition of one's basic nature.

essence love   Warmth and openness unimpeded by bias or conditioning.

gewa   Tibetan. An adjective used to describe something that empowers or strengthens; often translated as "virtuous."

Glossary

Kagyu A Tibetan Buddhist lineage based on the oral transmission of teachings from master to student; from the Tibetan words *ka*, meaning "speech," and *gyu*, meaning "lineage."

Karmapa The head of the Karma Kagyu lineage of Tibetan Buddhism.

khata Tibetan. A white silk scarf symbolizing an offering of the heart.

kṣānti Sanskrit. Tibetan: *zöpa*. Patience, the third *pāramitā*.

lhen-kyé-ma-rig-pa Tibetan. A fundamental ignorance that emerges simultaneously with sentience and that leads to confusion and uncertainty about the way things are.

lung Tibetan. An energy force in the subtle body that carries the *tigle* through the *tsa*. See also subtle body, *tigle*, *tsa*.

mantra Sanskrit. The repetition of special combinations of ancient syllables.

nying-jé Tibetan. Noble heart.

Nyingma The oldest of the four main lineages of Tibetan Buddhism; from a Tibetan term that may be roughly translated as "the old ones."

ö-sel-wa Tibetan. Most commonly translated as "luminosity," a fundamental capacity to illuminate—or shed light on—our experiences and thus to know or be aware of them.

pāramitā Sanskrit. Tibetan: *pa-rol-tu-chin-pa*. Often translated as "perfection," in the sense of being the most open, kind, and intelligent qualities that we can cultivate on the path toward absolute *bodhicitta*. A more literal translation means "going beyond" or "crossing to the other shore."

prajñā Sanskrit. Tibetan: *sherab*. Wisdom, the discerning capability of the mind. The sixth *pāramitā*.

relative *bodhicitta* The intention, within the relativistic framework of self and other, to raise all sentient beings to the level at which they recognize their buddha nature. See also absolute *bodhicitta*, application *bodhicitta*, aspiration *bodhicitta*, *bodhicitta*.

relative reality The moment-by-moment experience of endless changes and shifts of thoughts, emotions, and sensory perceptions.

241

samsara   Sanskrit. Tibetan: *khorlo*. Wheel. In Buddhist terms, the wheel of relative reality.

sem   Tibetan. That which knows; that which feels.

shamata   Sanskrit. Calm abiding practice; simply allowing the mind to rest calmly as it is. See also *shinay*.

shezhin   Tibetan. Knowing one's own awareness. The attentive aspect of consciousness through which we observe the mind itself in the act of being aware of an object.

shinay   Tibetan. Calm abiding practice; simply allowing the mind to rest calmly as it is. See also *shamata*.

sīla   Sanskrit. Tibetan: *tsultrim*. Discipline, the second *pāramitā*. Also translated as "ethics," "morality," or "moral discipline."

subtle body   Best understood as the place where emotions emerge and abide, asserting an often tangible effect on the physical body.

śūnyatā   Sanskrit. Tibetan: *tongpa-nyi*. Both words are commonly translated as "emptiness." The Sanskrit word *śūnya* is "zero," an infinitely open space or background that allows for anything to appear. The Tibetan word *tongpa* means "empty" in the sense of a basis of experience that is beyond our ability to perceive with our senses, to describe, to name, or to capture in a nice, tidy concept.

sugatagarbha   Sanskrit. The essence of one who has "gone to" bliss. See also buddha nature, *tathagatagarbha*.

tathagatagarbha   Sanskrit. The essence of one who is "thus-gone." See also buddha nature, *sugatagarbha*.

terma   Tibetan. Literally, "treasure" or "treasures." Refers specifically to the hidden teachings of great meditation masters to be discovered in later centuries, during times of great need.

tertön   Tibetan. "Treasure finder." A great meditation master who has rediscovered hidden teachings.

tigle   Tibetan. Literally "drops" or "droplets." In Tibetan Buddhism these are considered "sparks of life." See also *lung*, subtle body, *tsa*.

tokden   Tibetan. A meditation master who has spent long years in solitary retreat perfecting his or her practice.

tonglen   Tibetan. "Sending and taking." The practice of sending all one's happiness to other sentient beings and taking in their suffering.

tsa   Tibetan. The channels in the subtle body through which energy flows. See also *lung*, subtle body, *tigle*.

tulku   Tibetan. An enlightened master who has chosen to reincarnate in human form.

vipaśyanā   Sanskrit. Tibetan: *lhaktong*. Clear seeing; seeing things as they truly are. Often loosely translated as "insight."

vīrya   Sanskrit. Tibetan: *tsondru*. Diligence, perseverance, effort, zeal. The fourth *pāramitā*.

For Further Reading

Adeu Rinpoche. *Freedom in Bondage: The Life and Teachings of Adeu Rinpoche*. Translated by Erick Pema Kunsang and compiled by Marcia Binder Schmidt. Hong Kong: Rangjung Yeshe Publications, 2011.

The Dhammapada. Translated by Eknath Easwaran. Tomales, CA: Nilgiri Press, 1985.

Kongtrul, Jamgön. *The Torch of Certainty*. Translated by Judith Hanson. Boston: Shambhala, 1977.

Śāntideva. *The Bodhicaryāvtāra*. Translated by Kate Crosby and Andrew Skilton. New York: Oxford University Press, 1995.

Tsoknyi Rinpoche. *Carefree Dignity*. Compiled and translated by Erick Pema Kunsang and Marcia Binder Schmidt. Edited by Kerry Morgan. Kathmandu: Rangjung Yeshe Publications, 1998.

———. *Fearless Simplicity*. Compiled and translated by Erick Pema Kunsang and Marcia Binder Schmidt. Edited by Kerry Morgan. Kathmandu: Rangjung Yeshe Publications, 2003.

Tulku Urgyen Rinpoche. *As It Is*. Vol. 1. Translated by Erik Pema Kunsang. Compiled by Marcia Binder Schmidt. Edited by Kerry Morgan. Boudhanath, Hong Kong, & Esby: Rangjung Yeshe Publications, 1999.

———. *As It Is*. Vol. 2. Translated by Erik Pema Kunsang. Compiled by Marcia Binder Schmidt. Edited by Kerry Morgan. Boudhanath, Hong Kong, & Esby: Rangjung Yeshe Publications, 2000.

For Further Reading

Yongey Mingyur Rinpoche with Eric Swanson. *The Joy of Living: Unlocking the Secret and Science of Happiness*. New York: Harmony Books, 2007.

———. *Joyful Wisdom: Embracing Change and Finding Freedom*. New York: Harmony Books, 2009.

Acknowledgments

For their inspiration and instruction, I would like to thank every one of my teachers, including my father, Tulku Urgyen Rinpoche; my grandfather, Tashi Dorje; Dilgo Khyentse Rinpoche; Adeu Rinpoche; Nyoshul Khen Rinpoche; Tselwang Rindzin; and many of my tutors and the *tokdens* at Tashi Jong. I would also like to thank my brother, Yongey Mingyur Rinpoche, for his encouragement and support, as well as my mother, my wife, and my daughters. I would especially like to thank Tashi Lama, who has, through his own brilliance, offered assistance in ways I cannot even begin to count.

I would also like to offer my gratitude to the various people who have given so generously to the organizations that have supported my work—especially Carole Bishop, Deborah Easley, Alfred Graf, Sandra Hammond, and Esteban and Tressa Hollander. I would like to thank the translators who have served throughout the years as transmitters of the Buddha's teachings on my behalf, particularly Gerardo Abboud and Erik Pema Kunsang. I also want to thank Laurie Lange, who has worked tirelessly transcribing the teachings I've given, and Sherab Chödzin Kohn, who began to put the teachings on essence love into book form.

Of course, this manuscript would not have come to light without the help of my agent, Emma Sweeney, who has supported this book as it has evolved; my editor, Julia Pastore, who has offered tremendously helpful comments and suggestions along the way; and the entire staff of the Crown Publishing Group, who have been extremely enthusiastic and supportive.

There are so many other people who have contributed to this book in a variety of ways. It would almost require another book to list all of their names, but I'd especially like to thank Tara Bennett-Goleman, Pedro Beroy, Owsley Brown, Richard Gere, Daniel Goleman, Neil Hogan, Michael Kunkel, and Sharon Salzberg for their kindness and generosity; Cortland Dahl, for his close reading of the manuscript and many helpful suggestions; and Martha Boyden, who opened her lovely home in Italy to Eric and me at a particularly important time. To the many others—you know who you are and how great a contribution you've made. May your spark brighten and your love and compassion continue to grow!

Index

Index

Index

Index

Index

Index

Index

About the Authors

Born in 1966 in Nubri, Nepal, Tsoknyi Rinpoche is one of the most renowned teachers of Tibetan Buddhism trained outside of Tibet. Deeply versed in both the practical and philosophical disciplines of Tibetan Buddhism, he is beloved by students around the world for his accessible style, his generous and self-deprecating humor, and his deeply personal, compassionate insight into human nature. The married father of two daughters, Rinpoche nevertheless manages to balance family life with a demanding schedule of teaching around the world, and overseeing two nunneries in Nepal, one of the largest nunneries in Tibet, and more than fifty practice centers and hermitages in the eastern region of Tibet. More information about Tsoknyi Rinpoche, his teachings, and his activities can be found at www.tsoknyirinpoche.org.

Eric Swanson is coauthor, with Yongey Mingyur Rinpoche, of the *New York Times* bestseller *The Joy of Living* and its follow-up volume, *Joyful Wisdom*. A graduate of Yale University and the Juilliard School, he is the author of several works of fiction and nonfiction. After converting to Buddhism in 1995, he co-wrote *Karmapa, The Sacred Prophecy*, a history of the Karma Kagyu lineage, and authored *What the Lotus Said*, a memoir of his journey to eastern Tibet.